EGYPT

Text by
CLAUDIO BAROCAS

Foreword by
OSCAR NIEMEYER

MONUMENTS OF CIVILIZATION

EGYPT

MADISON SQUARE PRESS
GROSSET & DUNLAP

Publishers New York

For permission to reprint the translated excerpts from the ancient Egyptian texts, we gratefully acknowledge the following:

R. O. Faulkner, *The Ancient Egyptian Pyramid Texts* (1969). By permission of the Clarendon Press, Oxford. [AEPT]

Selections from *Ancient Near Eastern Texts Relating to the Old Testament*, ed. James B. Pritchard (3rd edn., with Supplement, copyright © 1969 by Princeton University Press), pp. 5, 212, 243–244, 365, 377, 412, 419–420, 424, 441–442, translated by John A. Wilson. Reprinted by permission of Princeton University Press. [ANET]

Selections from *The Ancient Egyptians: A Sourcebook of Their Writings*, by Adolph Erman (Harper Torchbooks, 1966). Reprinted by permission of Harper & Row, Publishers, Inc. [AESW]

Selections from *Ancient Records of Egypt*, by James Henry Breasted (Copyright 1906 by The University of Chicago Press). Reprinted by permission of The University of Chicago Press. [ARE]

Selections from *Hieratic Papyri in the British Museum*, 3rd Series, edited by Alan H. Gardiner (1935). By courtesy of the Trustees of the British Museum. [HPBM]

From "The Religion of the Poor in Ancient Egypt" by Battiscombe Gunn, in the *Journal of Egyptian Archaeology*, Vol. III, 1916. By permission of the Egypt Exploration Society. [JEA]

A MADISON SQUARE PRESS BOOK
First published in the United States in 1972
by Grosset & Dunlap, 51 Madison Avenue, New York 10010

English translation copyright © 1972 by Mondadori, Milano-Kodansha, Tokyo; originally published in Italian under the title "Grandi Monumenti: Egitto," copyright © 1970 by Mondadori, Milano-Kodansha, Tokyo; copyright © 1970 by Kodansha Ltd., Tokyo, for the illustrations; copyright © 1970 by Mondadori, Milano-Kodansha, Tokyo, for the text.

Editorial Director
GIULIANA NANNICINI
American Editorial Supervisor
JOHN BOWMAN

CONTENTS

FOREWORD

A modern architect confronts the pyramids: this could promise a fascinating, stimulating subject for meditation. But an architect is also a human being; when confronted with such testimony of a distant past, he feels first of all that he is a man like everyone else and only secondarily an artist or engineer.

Egypt today still conjures up for us images of great pyramids, those grandiose symbols of our most ancient history. The evocative vision of the Giza pyramids, which seem to rise from the desert in perfect geometric forms, provoked in me the same intense emotion as it does in any visitor. It was a July afternoon, and the declining sun made the pyramids golden, tracing their immense black shadows on the sand, casting a magic spell over me. The pyramids were the concrete expression of a particular human situation: once they represented the absolute power of the Pharaohs, but they had been created by human labor, the great "motor" of four thousand years ago. A Stone Age land, an agricultural country with very limited technical means, had been able to create monuments that have challenged the ages. But this nation of farmers had a great instrument at its disposal: the organization of human labor. So it is that the temples, pyramids, and other monuments of ancient Egypt symbolize the pharaonic power that assigned to itself divine attributes, but they are also a testimony to the patient, infinite, resigned, capacity for work on the part of hundreds of thousands of ordinary human beings.

And then I thought, with a mixture of pain and pride, of how man has changed the face of the earth during his sojourn on this planet: pain, because of the fatigue and suffering that this transformation has cost; pride, because only man among all living creatures has left such a lasting imprint of himself.

Every stage in the long course of human history is marked by some form of tangible evidence, of which architecture constitutes a fundamental portion. Testimony of a civilization, visual expression of a particular conception of the world, the monuments of ancient Egypt tell a story that lasted for millenniums. A monumentality never surpassed; an absolute, formal exactitude; a technical capacity for construction of the highest order; a perfect integration of architecture and decorative elements, whether sculpture, painting, or inscriptions — all contribute to an effect that, over the centuries, has impressed even the least tutored visitor to Egypt.

Of course, questions rush to the mind. An architect who believes in man's potential and courage, in his creative capacity, cannot but ask himself, "Why?". Why did the Egyptians continue to build for some 2500 years monuments that to us seem to be the product of a single architectural age? And what is the real significance of these ancient temples and pyramids?

Once we have raised these questions, any considerations about the technical capacities of the ancient Egyptians become less important. In fact, a civilization that wants to present an image of itself always finds the means, no matter what level of technical capacity it has reached. And it is the analysis of these monuments that allows us to understand the society that created them. How were these projects organized? With the great technical means that today allow us to take apart and transport whole temples — as we have done with those threatened by the waters from the new Aswan Dam — why do we today not think of constructing pyramids?

The author of this book has undertaken to answer these and other questions posed by the monuments of ancient Egypt. I think he has approached both the monuments and the history of ancient Egypt with precise attention and profound understanding. In so doing, he helps us better to appreciate the beauty of these monuments that stand as witnesses, not only to man's toil but also to his greatness.

Oscar Niemeyer.

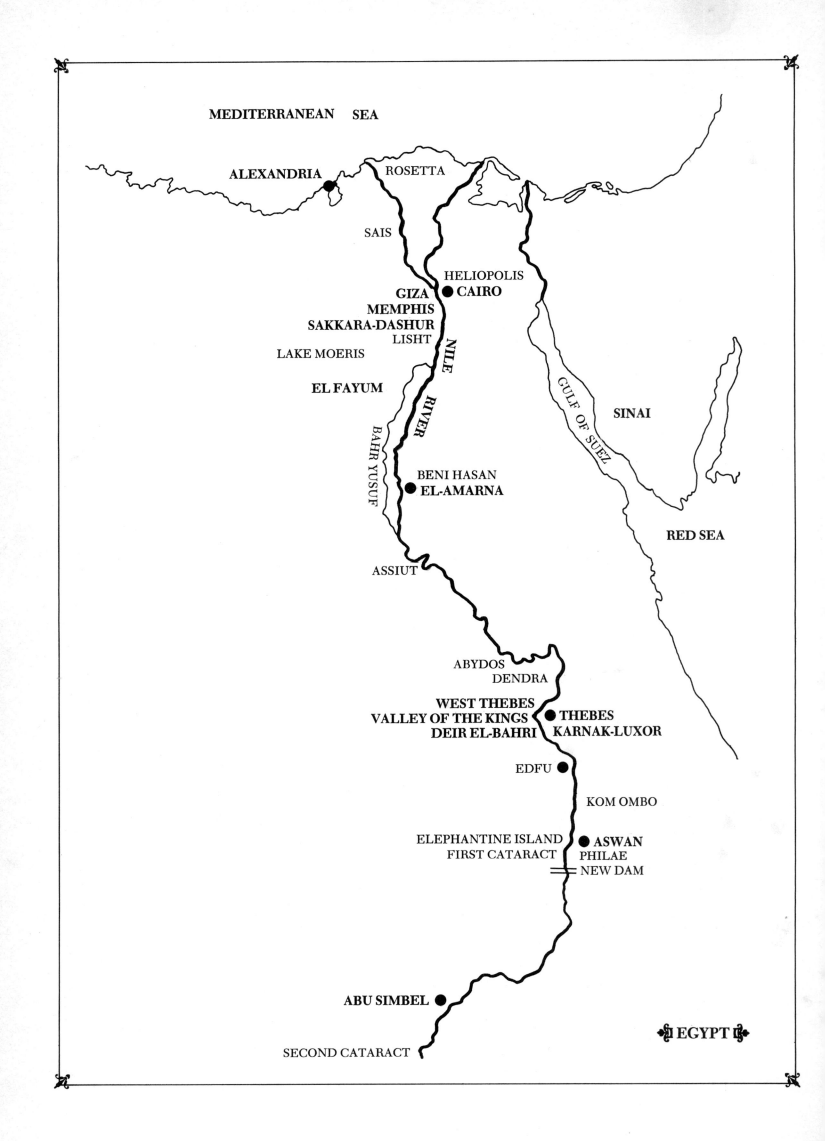

MEDITERRANEAN   SEA

ALEXANDRIA

ROSETTA

SAIS

HELIOPOLIS

GIZA
MEMPHIS
SAKKARA-DASHUR
LISHT

LAKE MOERIS

EL FAYUM

CAIRO

NILE

RIVER

BAHR YUSUF

GULF OF SUEZ

SINAI

RED SEA

BENI HASAN
EL-AMARNA

ASSIUT

ABYDOS
DENDRA

WEST THEBES
VALLEY OF THE KINGS
DEIR EL-BAHRI

THEBES
KARNAK-LUXOR

EDFU

KOM OMBO

ELEPHANTINE ISLAND
FIRST CATARACT

ASWAN
PHILAE
NEW DAM

ABU SIMBEL

EGYPT

SECOND CATARACT

INTRODUCTION

From the Nile's first cataract, a rocky outcrop near present-day Aswan, to the Mediterranean Sea, the river flows about seven hundred miles. For the first six hundred miles north of the rapids, the Nile is flanked on the east by rocky, rugged desert hills that separate it from the Red Sea. To the west are the soft, sandy hills that form the easternmost fringe of the Sahara Desert. About one hundred miles from the Mediterranean, the Nile splits into many branches and spreads out like a fan to form the Delta, a fertile, swampy area that becomes uninhabitable as it merges with the sea. Dry trade winds, blowing persistently southward, dominate this whole region, and although the winds make for an eternally blue sky and an attractive climate, they have also helped to create the desert that borders the Nile. Given these conditions, human beings can exist only along the immediate banks of the river, and that is precisely where the civilization of ancient Egypt took root and flourished.

Herodotus, the 5th century B.C. Greek historian, called Egypt "the gift of the Nile." At the simplest level, the mass of Egyptians were dependent on the river, using the mud along its shores to build their houses, or cutting the papyrus in its marshes to make everything from rope to writing paper. Ultimately, Egypt's economy, its social and political structures, and even its cultural values, were shaped by the river. And in the most literal sense, Egypt is an extended oasis that owes its existence to the waters of the Nile.

Every year around the middle of July, the water level of the Nile along the valley floor begins to rise slowly. The waters swell from the spring rains and melting snow in the equatorial region where the sources of the Nile are located — in the mountains of Ethiopia and Uganda. Before the construction of the Aswan dams in modern times, which now regulate the flow of the water from Aswan to the Mediterranean, this section of the Nile reached its maximum level between August and November. Then the waters slowly receded, leaving a residual deposit of mineral-rich mud and silt on a strip that ranged from a few yards to a few miles at the widest.

Except for this annual deposit, there was barely any naturally fertile earth in Egypt. The Egyptian countryside is composed predominantly of limestone and sand, with none of the variety of landscape — the pastures, brushland, and woods — that one finds in Europe or the Americas. In Egypt there is either cultivable land, or desert. And until quite recently, no one could be sure where the boundaries would be until the flooding subsided. Premature or excessive flooding could hinder the fertilization process or wash away any settlements; insufficient flooding could mean drought and famine. Left to itself, the river's rich deposit would quickly dry into an arid, stony surface.

Such were the tenuous conditions of life in ancient Egypt: the very factors that made the land a seeming paradise also kept the people perpetually on the edge of disaster. The ancient Egyptians could not simply sit back and wait for the floods to renew the land; they had to devise means to control the amount and distribution of these waters. The first people to settle the Nile Valley probably came as early as 8000 B.C., but they were semi-nomadic hunters and food-gatherers. Eventually, scattered tribes must have merged to form more stable villages and to cooperate in irrigation and farming projects that made the best use of the river's annual inundation. Strong local leaders extended their influence over neighboring villages, unifying them into a society that permitted the diversification of labor.

The rich and well-developed Neolithic culture of Egypt has bequeathed precious testimony of this phase, especially in its stone tools and stone or ceramic vases. The perfection of these vases clearly demonstrates the existence of master craftsmen. Such specialization is possible only in a society that has a sufficient surplus of goods necessary to maintain those who are not directly engaged in producing essential commodities. But the surplus could not have been that large during those early centuries, and conflicting interests probably led to the formation of opposing groups or power blocs. Local village leaders must have struggled with regional chieftains for position and privileges until one was sufficiently powerful to extend his jurisdiction over the whole Delta region, while another dominated the southern region to the first cataract.

The next stage came when one man unified these two territories, the upper and lower regions of the Nile Valley. Around 3100 B.C., the semi-legendary Menes became the first king of Upper and Lower Egypt; in this role he is known historically as Narmer. King Narmer established what were to remain the geographical boundaries of Egypt for many centuries to come, and created a single administration to govern the land and to levy taxes. Such enterprise demanded strong leadership, and with King Narmer there began to evolve the kind of ruler that culminated in the great pharaohs. (The actual title, Pharaoh — meaning "great house" — was not used until many centuries later.) Such a king assumed the function of a god on earth as well as guarantor of order. Above all, since Egypt was always dependent upon its agricultural economy, the king had to inspire the organization for controlling the river's waters and cultivating the land.

During the first stage that Narmer inaugurated, there was no "empire," no impulse to expand beyond the country's natural boundaries. Because the ruling class of early Egypt felt bound by the social and administrative institutions that it helped to create, the system rapidly achieved an equilibrium and stability that is rare in any age. Ancient Egypt was self-contained; indeed, Egypt was isolated in two senses: the physical barriers of desert and hills that discouraged invaders also cut the Egyptians off from the world at large. It is not surprising that the ancient Egyptians, whom we know mainly through the surviving remains of the ruling class, considered themselves to be the only truly civilized beings on the earth.

The Nile, the desert, human labor: these formed the base of ancient Egyptian culture; and taken together, they explain why a unified state developed here so early in history. (Contemporaneous developments in Mesopotamia differed to the extent that the people there were neither as restricted nor as linked by the environment.) In effect, human survival required the formation of agricultural communities along the Nile. Such communities provided access to human labor in sufficient quantities to ensure the security and stability of life in the area. Regulating the flow of Nile waters by dikes and canals, digging and maintaining irrigation ditches, reclaiming and cultivating thousands of acres of land — such enormous projects required the rapid and efficient mobilization of large, well-integrated groups working together for a common purpose. It was this need for collective action that spurred the growth of civilization along the Nile. To cite but one specific offshoot, careful observation of the annual cycle of the river's water-flow and dependent agricultural practices led the Egyptians to develop relatively early a calendar that is still the basis of our calendar.

Once these basic factors are grasped, a whole series of others will become evident when we concentrate on the monuments of ancient Egypt. Here it would be well to stress a more general characteristic of this country's history. One often encounters the claim that the pharaonic civilization was extremely static, that it continued unchanged for centuries. Such immutability is assigned no particular virtue; indeed, a certain criticism is usually implied, even though we ourselves may long for some greater stability in our own institutions. Actually it is only in comparison with our own fast-moving and ever-changing Western culture that ancient Egypt seems static and slow-moving. Within the context of its own period and in relation to its own institutions, we shall discover considerable dynamism and diversity in Egypt's development.

In the centuries immediately following King Narmer's unification of Egypt — that is, in the third millennium B.C. — the eastern part of the Mediterranean was still in the Stone Age. Those who associate the "Stone Age" with crude cave men should remember that it was in the last phase of the Stone Age, and along the eastern shores of the Mediterranean, that metallurgy developed. It was also during this Neolithic period that a change occurred that would decisively affect all ancient cultures. This was the development of specialized handicraft production. We have already noted that specialization of labor — such as vase-making — creates conditions for the formation of social classes; some of these will perform functions not directly connected with food production — such as expending more care on vases than their use requires. With the use of metals — initially copper, and then bronze — and the development of the secondary tasks associated with metallurgy, a new system of social relationships was born.

It is in this setting that Egypt must be considered. The unified central administration was able to integrate its environmental, as well as its societal, resources. Such a state is unlikely to favor the growth of trade with other nations. It would be more apt to develop its irrigation projects and improve its tax systems. Moreover, all this was carried out in such a way as to maintain the internal balance that guarantees the state's continued existence. Change is discouraged because it threatens this balance, and consequently, weakens the administration.

We may accept, then, that the same factors that made human life possible in the prehistoric Nile Valley before 3000 B.C. paved the way for the type of civilized society that subsequently prospered there. But when conditions in the eastern Mediterranean changed from about 1500 B.C. on, Egypt began to lose its place as the supreme representative of a certain type of world. The emergence of more aggressive peoples and the use of iron were among the factors that led to new internal and external relationships. The pharaoh and his class of functionaries were deprived of the support that had sustained them for centuries. The mass of Egyptians, completely divorced from a sense of common destiny, were unable to reorganize themselves on any new footing.

So it was that when the Greeks made direct contact with the culture of the Nile Valley (and we are here thinking of Herodotus in the 5th century B.C.), they had a strong sensation of encountering an illustrious and admirable country, but one that was old, living merely on its past. It is the youth, maturity, and decline of Egypt, as reflected in its great monuments, that we must now examine in detail.

THE OLD KINGDOM

The Meaning of the Pyramids

Anyone who has ever let his imagination travel through time has been intrigued by the great pyramids of Egypt. Amateur historians are quick to associate the famous pyramids of Giza with absolute despotism or the oppression of the masses, while popular films or stories about ancient Egypt usually include spectacular scenes depicting the construction of the pyramids. Yet, the pyramids are among the least comprehensible of all the great monuments left to us from ancient cultures. When referring to ancient Egypt, everyone is ready to speak of slaves sweating under the lash or of blind faith in the divinity of kings — always with the pyramids in mind. We lack the evidence to support or refute most such claims. In fact, they are assumptions we put forth to explain why an entire nation should have undertaken such an immense task merely to bury the remains of a man.

Clearly, we shall not get very far if we persist in carrying out investigations along such lines. It seems equally futile to argue over how, with their limited technology, the ancient Egyptians could have placed millions of limestone blocks, weighing many tons, one on top of the other. All we can say for certain is that the great pyramids exist, that they were built long ago, and that we — with all our technology — do not construct pyramids simply because we would consider it a waste of time and effort. But technology is the expression of the society, and this applies to ancient Egypt as well as to any modern culture. It is with this assumption that we do best to direct our search for a solution to the pyramids, leaving aside for the moment considerations of the utility of such monuments.

The inexhaustible speculations over the pyramids of Egypt are encouraged by many factors. The sheer imposing bulk of some of the pyramids, particularly the three at Giza, is enough to justify the most daring flights of fantasy. Then, too, they are so greatly separated in time from our world, and our knowledge is based upon comparatively recent testimony that has no direct connection with the builders themselves. The pyramids seem to have risen in a vacuum, without precedents or successors. Little wonder that they continue to loom as mysterious, almost frightening forms, eluding the rational mind. Faced with such limitations, archaeologists probably have taken the best approach. Archaeological research has played a predominant part in casting light on these shadowy monuments, and hardly a month passes without new discoveries or deductions that reveal further precious details. We shall be turning, therefore, to the archaeologists to see what they have uncovered.

For now, we may accept that the Egyptian pyramid was a tomb — or, more precisely, the part that encloses or covers a tomb, much like a

mausoleum. This type of tomb was used in Egypt for the kings during the Old and Middle Kingdoms; in the New Kingdom it was used for nobles and high officials. This means that for a period of nearly 1500 years, the pyramid was associated with a society's ideas about the burial of the dead. But if we know why the pyramids were built, we still are left wondering why the Egyptians adopted such a form. And since pyramids vary in height from a few yards to — in the case of the largest, the Pyramid of Cheops at Giza — about 150 yards, simple measurements tell us nothing. More significant is the fact that we have no ancient Egyptian document that speaks explicitly of the connection between the pyramids and burial customs. This, however, far from surprising us, is further proof that the Egyptians took their pyramids as much for granted as a modern Christian does the cross over a tomb. Pyramids were such a natural part of the scene that ancient Egyptians felt no need to comment on them.

Memphis: Capital of the Two Lands

The Egyptian nation is so old, moreover, that many generations of Egyptians lived out their lives before any pyramids rose on the horizon. The construction of the first pyramids, in fact, coincides with the founding of what is known historically as the Old Kingdom, which began about 2686 B.C. with the Third Dynasty. Before that, the first two dynasties of eighteen kings had ruled Egypt for about four hundred years. For thousands of years before that, people had inhabited the Nile Valley, passing through the Neolithic "revolution" along with other peoples of the Fertile Crescent. Gradually the country became polarized around the two naturally distinct geopolitical entities: Upper Egypt (roughly, the Nile Valley between the first cataract and the Delta), and lower Egypt (essentially the Delta). The leader of Upper Egypt wore a white cone-shaped crown (much like a bishop's miter), while the ruler of Lower Egypt wore a red crown (shaped somewhat like a high-backed chair).

Then, about 3100 B.C., Menes, a leader of Upper Egypt, extended his jurisdiction into the Delta. He not only united the country but also founded the first of Egypt's many dynasties. It was Menes, too, who started the tradition of the Double Crown — the white crown inserted in the red crown. This signified his sovereignty over both parts of the country. After Menes — or Narmer, as he became known — the pharaoh was known as "Lord of the Two Lands." King Narmer led Egypt out of the dim shadows of prehistory to the edge of civilization. Among his many achievements was the creation of the unified nation's first capital city, about twenty miles below the apex of the Delta (and southwest of modern Cairo). Located on the west bank of the Nile, this city was at first called White Wall, in reference to the white wall that surrounded its citadel, but later it came to be known as Memphis. Today, this city has all but vanished. Only a few ruins scattered over a twenty-mile radius bear witness to the existence of this once great city.

Basically there is one reason why little or nothing remains of Memphis — and, for that matter, of the other great cities of ancient Egypt. They were located, for obvious reasons, along the arable strip of the river valley, and virtually all the buildings were built of mud bricks. The lack of available space, together with the need to raise the ground in order to withstand the annual floods, determined the vertical growth of the cities. "Vertical growth" does not refer to multi-storied structures, but rather to periodic rebuilding of houses in the same place,

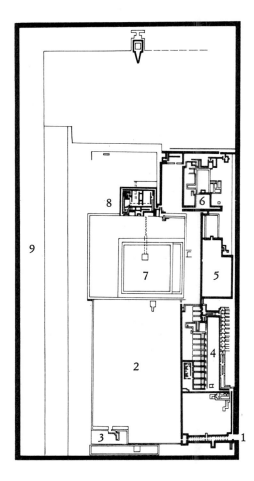

Sakkara: Mortuary Complex of King Djoser
1 Entrance and colonnade
2 Southern courtyard
3 Southern tomb
4 Courtyard of the chapels
5–6 Eastern courtyards
7 Step Pyramid
8 Mortuary Temple
9 Storerooms

1. Sakkara: The south side of the Step Pyramid of King Djoser (Third Dynasty) as seen from the center of the southern courtyard.

using as foundations the remains of the pre-existing structures. In this way, little hills were formed, emerging from the flood waters like so many islets. The cities kept pace with the general process of elevation along the floor of the entire river valley. When abandoned by the inhabitants, these sites were invaded by the river waters and desert sands, eventually becoming sizable mounds. Such mounds — now known by their Arabic name, *tell* — are theoretically the pride and joy of modern archaeologists, holding forth the possibility of unearthing a center of habitation in which are preserved, layer upon layer in strict succession, the various periods of a city's life.

In fact, Egyptologists rarely enjoy this pleasure, especially when they come to ancient cities such as Memphis. In many cases, the ancient center has continued to be inhabited up to the present and thus would require the demolition of inhabited houses. Beyond that, the infiltration of the Nile into the lower, oldest levels of tells has destroyed most of those remains which were made of perishable material, including the mud-brick structures. Consequently, only the durable stone structures usually survive, and in ancient Egypt these were tombs and temples. This explains why we know so much about the places of burial and worship of the ancient Egyptians, and so little about where they lived.

But this accounts for only one half of our distorted view of ancient Egypt. The irrigated-inhabited area of the Nile Valley varies continuously in its dimensions, but except in the Delta region, one need not travel far to reach the desert, either to the east or to the west. The ancient Egyptians thus had at their disposal an area easily within reach and with practically unlimited space in which to place their tombs. And the desert area did not use valuable cultivable land. So it is that, if almost all the ancient Egyptians' cities have vanished, their cemeteries have survived for millenniums, often in excellent condition. Moreover, the dry environment and the sterility of the desert sands have preserved not only mineral substances, such as stone, metal, or paint, but also organic materials as well. Certain objects of wood or papyrus have survived remarkably intact. Since most of these remains have been found in cemeteries, we have wrongly concluded that ancient Egyptians were ready to sacrifice everything for a worthy tomb.

This explains how a center as large and important as Memphis could disappear, even though it grew in the centuries after Narmer to become the greatest city in Egypt and thrived for almost four thousand years. Such a city would have necessarily impressive cemeteries, and the tombs of ancient Memphis extend for many miles from the edge of the cultivated land into the desert, from Abu Rawash north of Giza to Medum in the South and include such famous monuments as those at Sakkara and Dashur. These names signify a precious mine of the most diverse information about the earliest phase of Egyptian civilization.

The Sakkara Complex

Once again, we must start by dispelling a false impression: the tomb of an ancient Egyptian, especially that of a royal personage, did not consist only of a pyramid. The pyramid was really an inseparable part of a complex of structures used, as far as is known today, for such functions as the burial rites, the worship of the dead person, services for attendant gods, and for various other rituals and ceremonies. It would be more appropriate to speak not so much of pyramids as of mortuary complexes, even if in many cases only the pyramids remain.

The most ancient of these complexes that has survived — and almost certainly the first such ambitious complex anywhere in the world — is the one dedicated to King Djoser, an early ruler of the Third Dynasty that marks the beginning of the Old Kingdom. Djoser ruled Egypt from Memphis and was buried just west of the city, at a place now known as Sakkara. To this day, a visit to Sakkara is part of every complete tour of Egypt. The visitor approaches a long wall, extending north to south, constructed of limestone blocks, its face marked by alternating juts and recesses and by occasional small ramparts. This is the eastern wall of the great rectangular enclosure of the mortuary complex, at the center of which rises the pyramid in six "steps" to a height of about two hundred feet: this is the famed Step Pyramid that most people associate with Sakkara.

Along the enclosure wall — with a total perimeter of over a mile, and some thirty-three feet high — fourteen large gateways are spaced among the ramparts. But thirteen of these are false, or dummy, portals; only one, near the south corner of the east side, is a true gateway. Entering here, you pass along a corridor flanked by false columns to arrive at a large courtyard, south of the pyramid. North of the corridor and adjacent to the eastern enclosure wall, are a whole series of courtyards, chapels, and other structures. To the north of the Step Pyramid is another courtyard and the funerary temple, while to the west and along the entire length of the western boundary wall there are two parallel arcades (still covered with heaps of stone and sand). Finally, between the southern enclosure wall and the southern courtyard there is a tomb, a rectangular construction with an arched covering.

In addition to the complex visible above ground, there exists a whole series of shafts, galleries, and chambers cut out of the rock beneath the enclosure. And under the pyramid itself is the burial chamber that contained the remains of the pharaoh. Around this room there is a network of underground passages and corridors, some of which have walls decorated with relief carvings of King Djoser; other corridors contain thousands of vases carved from alabaster, serpentine, rock crystal, breccia, and other fine stones. Beneath the southern building there is a second burial chamber surrounded by a network of subterranean rooms similar to the ones beneath the Step Pyramid. Under the two western galleries, two parallel rows cut out of rock contain hundreds of corridors and rooms.

The essential elements of the Sakkara complex have been enumerated for several reasons. For one, it is the most ancient mortuary complex extant; it is also the only one that allows us to reconstruct more than a mere ground plan. Moreover, the Sakkara complex sheds vital light on a period of ancient Egypt about which we would otherwise know very little. Then, too, in certain other respects, Sakkara holds a special place among all the archaeological remains of ancient Egypt that are now available. So far as we know, it is, the first monument in any culture to have been completely conceived in stone. And — most remarkable — we even know the name of the person who, if not actually the architect who designed it, evidently coordinated the construction: Imhotep. We shall be hearing more about this legendary man later, but for now we can consider him the first non-royal *individual* to emerge out of ancient history.

What can we learn from an examination of the remains of the Sakkara complex? Take the element that first disturbs the modern

visitor: certain structures have no interior. They are facades, outside walls and doorways, but they have no interior rooms or corridors; the buildings consist merely of cores of brickwork with an outer casing of limestone blocks. This seems to suggest the same principle as the false gateways in the main enclosure wall.

Together, they provide our first hint of the symbolic nature of the whole complex: these "unreal" structures were for some spirit who would put them to a special use. We do not know precisely who or what this "spirit" was. There are few inscriptions in the Sakkara complex, but from later texts we deduce that this false element must have had something to do with the dead king's soul. Having left his body, the soul needed certain structures in order to survive. However, we must not think of some simple or direct relationship between the soul — or, better yet, a sort of immaterial "double" of the body (*ka*, in Egyptian) — and the structures designed for this "double." Some-

2. Sakkara: In the foreground is part of the mortuary temple of King Unas (Fifth Dynasty). In the background is the southern part of the enclosure wall of King Djoser's mortuary complex; behind it, to the left, is the superstructure of the southern tomb, while to the right is the entrance corridor, now protected by a modern roof. The Step Pyramid itself dominates the scene.

Dashur: The Bent Pyramid
(east-west cross-section)
1 Entrance
2 Mortuary chamber

3. Dashur: The southern side of the south pyramid of Sneferu (Fourth Dynasty), known as the Bent Pyramid because of its change in slope angles part way up the sides.

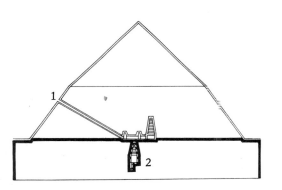

one might suggest, for instance, that the structures are false because the soul, being immaterial, could enter them all the same. But if the Egyptians had thought along these lines, most likely they would not have built anything: the buildings could have been as immaterial as the *ka*. The motivation for such unreal structures is more complicated.

Who has not fallen madly in love during adolescence? And who has not written the beloved's name time and again, filling up entire sheets of paper or tracing the name in the sand or on a foggy window pane? Instinctively, person, name, and written symbol are inseparably bound in our minds. So much so that, on an emotional level, writing a person's name is an evocation of that person; moreover, it is almost like setting that person out of time so that he or she might last forever.

Now, according to an Egyptian text (which has come down to us in a late version, although it probably dates back to the early dynasties), Ptah, the patron deity of Memphis, created the universe by listing one

by one the names of all its elements and creatures. We shall later see that this simple story provides the essential clue to many ancient Egyptian figurative representations as well as the inscriptions. What it signifies here is that certain ancient Egyptians believed that the word — spoken or written — had the force and reality of other works created by the gods or men. As mentioned, there are few literal inscriptions in the Sakkara complex, and these few are found only in the subterranean apartments. But following the story of Ptah, we can consider the entire Sakkara complex of King Djoser as a monumental inscription in which the buildings and various structures are themselves like hieroglyphic signs.

Now we can consider another factor: the use of stone. As mentioned earlier, the Sakkhara complex is the first monument known to have been conceived entirely in stone. But what do we possess of the Egypt

4. Dashur: The zone of the pyramids viewed from the north. In the foreground are the remains of the Old Kingdom mortuary structures. In the background are the two pyramids of King Sneferu: the Bent Pyramid on the left, the Red Pyramid on the right.

There came into being as the heart and there came into being as the tongue something in the form of Atum. The mighty Great One is Ptah, who transmitted life to all gods, as well as to their *ka*'s, through this heart, by which Horus became Ptah, and through this tongue, by which Thoth became Ptah.

Thus it happened that the heart and tongue gained control over every other member of the body, by teaching that he is in every body and in every mouth of all gods, all men, all cattle, all creeping things, and everything that lives, by thinking and commanding everything that he wishes.

His Ennead is before him in the form of teeth and lips. That is the equivalent of the semen and hands of Atum. Whereas the Ennead of Atum came into being by his semen and his fingers, the Ennead of Ptah, however, is the teeth and lips in this mouth, which pronounced the name of everything, from which Shu and Tefnut came forth, and which was the fashioner of the Ennead.

The sight of the eyes, the hearing of the ears, and the smelling the air by the nose, they report to the heart. It is this which causes every completed concept to come forth, and it is the tongue which announces what the heart thinks.

[ANET, p. 5]

before that time? A few of the tombs belonging to kings of the first two dynasties have been preserved. They consist of rooms built under ground, with walls of mud brick covered with painted wood or matting. Their superstructures, at least of those in the Sakkara area, consist of a rectangular core of mud bricks and an exterior wall (also of mud bricks) with rectangular juts and recesses, plastered and painted. Moreover — and we shall see the full importance of this later — from the beginning of the Second Dynasty the Egyptians developed the subterranean storerooms to the extent that the burial chamber is almost completely hidden.

In King Djoser's complex, we find the same storerooms, the same chambers, the same juts and recesses on the enclosure wall. But everything is now made of stone — relatively small limestone blocks (about 11 to 16 inches long and 8 inches high) — implying that the Egyptians were erecting on a more ambitious scale the structures that up to then they had traditionally made from mud bricks. This is the strongest evidence (if not outright proof) that all the monuments in the Sakkara enclosure are stone representations of once real structures that had previously been built of perishable materials.

Let us review the stone structures at Sakkara. They include two series of chapels that flank one of the courtyards north of the entrance colonnade, two buildings situated at the end of two other courtyards east of the pyramid, and the structure above a shaft with a mortuary chamber at the southern end of the enclosure. Focusing on the reconstructed exterior walls of these buildings, we become aware of the consistency of the two "sets": one type of chapel west of the courtyard and another to the east; two different buildings for the two eastern courtyards, one to the north and the other to the south; and the southern tomb matched by the great Step Pyramid.

According to the interpretation accepted by many Egyptologists, these structures "spelled out" a concept typical of ancient Egyptian culture. We have traced the unification of Egypt and Lower Egypt under King Narmer, at which time there were two separate administrative centers and two relatively distinct cultures. Exactly what transpired in the four centuries between King Narmer and King Djoser is not known. But whatever the social, political, economic, cultural or other developments during those centuries and all the centuries that followed, Egyptians never lost their awareness of their nation as the fusion of "the two lands." And so, when they came to build the mortuary complex for Djoser at Sakkara, they built two of everything: two chapels representing the sanctuaries typical of the two kingdoms, two buildings with courtyards to represent the palaces in which the king exercised sovereignty over the two lands, and two tombs for the man whose spirit watched over Upper Egypt and Lower Egypt.

The Message of Sakkara

Some of these explorations of the Sakkara complex are hypotheses and interpretations. But what can be said for certain is that the stone buildings are modelled after those made from the perishable materials in which the king had carried out his royal functions on earth. Sakkara's symbolic "message" is that a mortuary complex did not so much relate to the Pharoah's afterlife as it allowed the dead sovereign to continue reigning even after death. This is the reason for the solid and

imperishable stone: to support the dead king's eternal reign. This evocative power of Sakkara grew out of the hieroglyphic aspect of the structures, already mentioned in connection with the myth of Ptah's creation of the world: if intellectual creation equaled reality, so too did the layout of the complex. Thus it seems justifiable to connect the Sakkara complex with the religious-governmental capital, Memphis. Many scholars, for example, see the enclosure wall of Djoser's mortuary complex as representing the "white wall" that once surrounded the citadel of Memphis.

The technical aspects of the Sakkara structures also yield valuable insights. Although it may at first seem strange, stone had been used for some construction in Egypt even before the introduction of mud bricks. Monuments built before the unification of the nation appear to have been composed of stone fragments mixed with a kind of mortar. Then, during the first two dynasties, the use of mud bricks prevailed. The architect of the Djoser complex, in turn, used limestone blocks joined by a good deal of mortar for the core of the pyramid. The new element was the facing blocks of Sakkara's structures, both of the

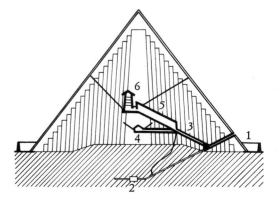

5. **Giza: The three great Fourth Dynasty pyramids as seen from the south. From left to right: the pyramid of Mycerinus, the pyramid of Chephren, and the pyramid of Cheops. Note the various smaller "satellite" pyramids, whose exact function is still obscure; the two at the far left are step pyramids, whose outer casing has been taken away.**

Giza: The Pyramid of Cheops (north-south cross-section)
1 *Entrance*
2 *First chamber*
3 *Ascending corridor*
4 *Second chamber*
5 *Great Gallery*
6 *Tomb chamber*

enclosure wall and the pyramid itself. For these, the Sakkara builders used a rather compact limestone that came from Tura (on the east bank of the Nile, opposite Sakkara); the blocks were perfectly dressed, or smoothed, so that they would fit together exactly with only a thin layer of mortar.

The facing blocks for the Djoser complex were brought to the site roughly shaped into squares, and were finished off during the construction at the site. This meant that, unlike standard bricks, the limestone blocks were not interchangeable; they were prepared to fit one specific place and no other. It can be noticed, however, that in the upper rows, especially in the enclosure wall, the builders tended to increase the size of the blocks, evidently with the intention of saving both time and labor. Finally, from traces left on the blocks as well as from the tools used by the stonecutters of the period, it has been possible to reconstruct the work procedures. The upper rows provide evidence, for instance, that the cutters changed from stone tools to copper chisels.

Now we are ready to expose the final clues to the true significance of this great complex: the first and most organic representation of

Egyptian royalty, the undisputed force that dominated the land from the Delta to the first cataract. If we examine Sakkara from this point of view, the use of stone acquires a more precise meaning. We have noted that, beyond the choice of such material for its permanency, the most apparent technical novelty of the complex was the precise shaping of the facing blocks. Beyond that, the enormous organization needed to extract and transport the stone was matched by the tremendous coordination of all the specialized skilled workers in the processing and working of the stone.

Obviously this great organization and coordination was possible only because there existed an already solidly established state that could maintain a great number of persons for the entire period of work. By this time — about 2680 B.C. — the basis of power in Egypt was control of agricultural production. We can safely assume that, with the Third Dynasty, royal power already had a most solid foundation. The more than 40,000 stone vases deposited in the subterranean storehouses are enough to convince us of this; they were filled with produce from the earth, another indication of the enormous accumulation of goods available in that period. This surplus, and this only, made the erection of the Sakkara complex possible. Incidentally, it is assumed that the same workmen were responsible for the magnificent stone vases made before and during the construction of the pyramid.

It is thus easy to see how the choice of stone for the Step Pyramid was not motivated exclusively by symbolic considerations, but had a more immediate, more tangible function. Utilizing so many skilled workers such as these stonecutters in the third millennium B.C. in Egypt implied the extension of the centralized power over the very part of the population that was potentially able to make itself independent — that is, less bound to external conditions than were the farmers. In this way, any latent social forces in the country were absorbed in advance. It was no accident that the production of stone vases declined sharply from the Third Dynasty onwards.

One final consideration: ancient Egyptian tradition has it that the mortuary complex of King Djoser was not only the first stone monument to be constructed but that it was constructed under the direction of Imhotep, the king's vizier, or chief minister. This same Imhotep was also celebrated in Egyptian tradition as a priest, astronomer, writer, wise man, and — perhaps most important — a physician. (Later, Imhotep was actually deified as a god of medicine.) During the excavations of the Sakkara enclosure, the base of a statue was found on which was inscribed, besides the name and titles of the pharaoh, those of Imhotep. This shows how the use of stone was linked with the very life of the ancient Egyptian state and to the essence of its culture.

Building the Fourth Dynasty Pyramids

During the entire Third Dynasty, the kings of Egypt continued to build step pyramids similar to Djoser's. In the Fourth Dynasty, the shape changed: the faces of the pyramids were no longer broken up into step sections but became smooth and perfectly triangular. And from a technical point of view, there was another novelty. The step pyramids were composed of a core of roughly square stone blocks, joined by mortar and set in rows that sloped toward the center, so that they converged at the center of the pyramid and were perpendicu-

A KING CLAIMS HIS RIGHT AS HORUS. FROM A PYRAMID TEXT

O Geb, Bull of the sky, I am Horus, my father's heir. I have gone and returned, the fourth of these four gods who have brought water, who have administered purification, who have rejoiced in the strength of their fathers; I desire to be vindicated by what I have done. I the orphan have had judgement with the orphaness, the Two Truths have judged, though a witness was lacking. The Two Truths have commanded that the thrones of Geb shall revert to me, so that I may raise myself to what I have desired. My limbs which were in concealment are reunited, and I join those who are in the Abyss, I put a stop to the affair in On, for I go forth today in the real form of a living spirit, that I may break up the fight and cut off the turbulent ones. I come forth, the guardian of justice, that I may bring it, it being with me; the wrathful ones bustle about for me and those who are in the Abyss assign life to me.
My refuge is my Eye, my protection is my Eye, my strength is my Eye, my power is my Eye. O you southern, northern, western, and eastern gods, honor me and fear me, for I have seated myself in the awning of the Two Courtyards, and that fiery snake the serpent would have burnt you, striking to your hearts. O you who would come against me in obstruction, come to me, come to me as friends, for I am the *alter ego* of my father, the blossom of my mother. I detest traveling in darkness, for then I cannot see, but fall upside down; I go forth today that I may bring justice, for it is with me, and I will not be given over to your flame, you gods.

[AEPT, p. 69]

lar to the outer steps. Such a method probably afforded the greatest solidity to the pyramid. The Fourth Dynasty pyramids, however, are composed of a core of large limestone blocks, squared with precision and laid in strictly horizontal rows, joined by a very thin layer of mortar. This method is probably connected with the new shape of the structure: the rows could no longer be perpendicular to the faces, as the slope, or incline, of the latter was too steep. Moreover, the weight of the blocks afforded greater stability to the structure as a whole.

The first differences we note between the pyramids of the Third and Fourth dynasties, therefore, are in the shape and in the technique of their construction. It is difficult in such cases to determine precisely how much the technical methods influenced the shape, or vice versa. But it is certain that building with the larger blocks meant a considerable saving of time and labor in the preparation of the material for construction. This saving, however, was taken up by the resultant need for a more complex organization of the transportation system. The construction of the Fourth Dynasty pyramids thus implies the use of a less specialized labor force than that used for the pyramids of the preceding dynasty, and the formation of a much smoother functioning administrative structure. By now, too, it should be clear why so much importance was attached to King Djoser's mortuary complex at Sakkara. If the Third Dynasty pyramids indicate that pharaonic power took root in the conflicts inherited from the preceding period — namely, the gradual centralization of the various forces in the country — the Fourth Dynasty pyramids are an indication of the total attainment of such power, and of the strengthening of those social institutions and structures that maintained its efficient functioning.

Indeed, one of the most developed characteristics of the Fourth Dynasty was its highly organized administrative structure. This structure was totally under the control of those connected with the royal court or, more to the point, dependent on the sovereign himself. During this period, no privilege was granted to dignitaries except by the pharaoh. We should keep this in mind whenever we marvel at the great pyramids: this centralized state organization was the most original and important accomplishment of Egyptian culture in the third millennium — much more so than the actual construction of the colossal stone monuments themselves.

Another point should be clarified once and for all: we do not know with absolute certainty how the Egyptians of the Fourth Dynasty built their various great pyramids. There are volumes of every kind of speculation dealing with this purely technical aspect, ranging from mysticism to science fiction. They all share one common trait: the unwillingness to consider ancient Egyptian society in its own terms. Each respective theory sees the technical problems as we would see them today. In so doing, all such theories violate one of the fundamental rules of any historical monument: it must be totally integrated with the economic and political aspects of the society that produced it.

We have been examining how the pyramids were completely integrated in the society that built them; the corollary of this is that they remain invaluable to us as a document of that society. The technical methods used in the pyramids' construction must be viewed in the same historical context. The pyramids were made possible only through rigorous central organization of all Egypt's resources. Why would the builders search for techniques to avoid using the only great force they had — namely, organization of many laborers. This was not because

the ancient Egyptians lacked the capacity for technical innovation, but rather because they already possessed the most effective instrument to serve their purposes. In this sense, human labor was the "machine" used in the disposition of those huge limestone or granite blocks; it is legitimate to speak of levers, ramps, or rollers, but not of machines in the modern sense of the word.

Still there is a very natural fascination about how the great pyramids were erected. Most theories — from the informed scholarly to the pseudo-inspired mystical — concentrate on the greatest of the Fourth Dynasty pyramids, the one at Giza built by King Cheops. (Or so he is best known to us through the Greek version of his name; his Egyptian name sounded more like Khufu.) Although Cheops' pyramid differs from the others in its vast dimensions and its internal arrangements, it does pose problems common to all the great pyramids. If we could account for how its 2,300,000 stone blocks — most weighing some two and a half tons, but some as much as fifteen tons — were put into place, then we will have probably explained the smaller pyramids. We offer here the explanation that is now most widely accepted by specialists in this subject.

Once the site for a pyramid was selected — in the case of Cheops' pyramid, a rocky mound north of Memphis — surveyors directed the cutting of a steplike terrace into the hill; this served as a foundation for the pyramid and was done with such precision that the thirteen-acre base, with sides some 755 feet long, had one corner only a half-inch higher

Giza: Chephren's Valley Temple
1 Entrances
2 Vestibule
3 Transverse hall
4 Longitudinal hall
5 Access way to the pyramid temple

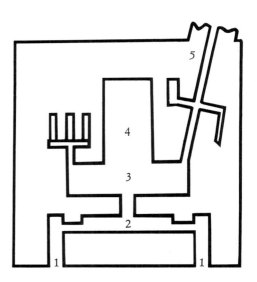

6. Giza: Chephren's mortuary complex seen from the east. In the foreground is the Valley Temple, flanked on the north by the Sphinx. In the center are the remains of the sacred way that led to the pyramid temple. The pyramid itself is distinguished by the section of outer casing that still remains at the peak. The pyramid of Mycerinus can be seen off to the left.

On the following pages:
7. Giza: The west side of the pyramid of Cheops, often known as the Great Pyramid. In the foreground are some Fourth Dynasty mastabas.

than another. The stone for the core was hewn on the spot; the facing blocks — a finer quality — were quarried at Tura, on the eastern side of the Nile (where the facing stones for the Sakkara complex had also been quarried). As the layers of the pyramid began to rise, four ramps — made of rubble and mud — were also built, each starting at one of the four corners and ascending alongside the unfinished facing blocks. The great stone blocks and other materials were hauled up three of these ramps (having a slope of about fifteen degrees) on sleds; the fourth ramp was used to bring down the empty sleds. No draft animals seem to have been used; to that extent, the popular image of hundreds of men straining at ropes pulling heavy stones is valid. At various stages in the process of transporting the stones from the quarry and on up the pyramid, rollers and lever-like prying tools were probably used; oil or water may also have been poured under the skids of the sleds to reduce friction. There has also been a serious suggestion that a weight-arm (like the shaduf still used in Egypt and other parts of the world to raise water) was used to lift the blocks up the sides, but this seems to involve as many problems as it solves. In any case, most scholars accept that the ramps and sleds were the principal devices used.

Eventually, the ramps went to the peak of the pyramid, where the capstone was put in place. Then, working downward, row by row, the workmen smoothed off the faces of the outer blocks to make the flat plane surface. As they did so, the ramps were removed and carted down until the pyramid stood free. Using such techniques, it has been estimated, would require only about 2,500–4,000 men on the pyramid itself; thousands of others, of course, would have been employed in the quarrying and trimming of stones and in the transportation system. Herodotus, the Greek historian, was told by the Egyptians when he visited the pyramids in the fifth century B.C. that 100,000 men worked on making a great pyramid, but this figure should not be taken literally — and certainly not as the number actively engaged at any given moment on making one pyramid. We must also assume that much of the labor force was seasonal, unskilled laborers and farmers left idle by the Nile's annual flooding — further evidence of how the technical details of pyramid-construction were inseparable from the total context of ancient Egypt.

The Pyramids at Dashur

As far as is known, the first sovereign of the Fourth Dynasty to be buried in a classic pyramid (that is, not a step pyramid such as those of the Third Dynasty) was Sneferu, founder of the Fourth Dynasty. There are at least two pyramids of his, situated at Dashur, south of Memphis and one of the many places that made up that city's vast cemetery. The southern pyramid of Sneferu is known as the Bent (or Rhomboid) Pyramid and the northern one as the Red Pyramid. These names have been applied in modern times simply for convenience. In the case of the former, the faces are not constructed on a single plane but undergo a distinct change in their slope half-way up: the latter derives its name from the reddish color of the calcareous local stone used for the core-blocks — and now exposed to the light. It seems certain that both monuments were built by Sneferu, but we do not know why he had two tombs built. Perhaps this is a case similar

8. Giza: The Sphinx (Fourth Dynasty) as seen from the east. Note, between the front paws, the stele bearing the inscription recounting the dream of Tuthmosis IV (Eighteenth Dynasty). In the background are Chephren's pyramid (left) and Cheops' pyramid (right).

to the complex of King Djoser at Sakkara, where the two tombs are similar in the arrangement of their subterranean rooms but differ in their superstructures.

Little has survived from the outer enclosures of the two pyramids at Dashur. It has been possible, however, to reconstruct the plan of the mortuary temple connected with the Bent Pyramid. This temple was rather simple, consisting basically of rooms used for the ritual of presenting offerings to the dead king to ensure his survival in the other life.

Inside the Bent Pyramid are two rooms, independent of each other but at right angles; both are reached by corridors, one beginning in

Sakkara: Pyramid of Unas
1 Entrance
2 Tomb chamber

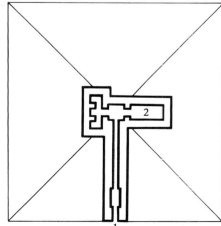

the northern wall of the pyramid, the other in the west wall. The Red Pyramid, as far as we know, was furnished with only one entrance; located in the northern wall, it gave access along a corridor to the mortuary chambers. The ancient Egyptians accepted that the entrance to the pyramid and access to the burial chamber could be used only up to the time that the king was buried within. Once the funeral rites were conducted, the door to the chamber was closed up by an enormous portcullis-type structure made of large stones, and the corridor was blocked up for most of its length by stone blocks. Finally, the entrance was covered by the same facing used for the entire pyramid.

The walls of the rooms are of particular interest. They consist of stone blocks placed one upon the other in rows that jut out slightly the higher they go, so that the two long walls eventually meet at a peak (forming what is known as a corbeled vault). Since the projection of each row is minimal, the height of the ceiling is considerable — a maximum of about twenty-seven yards in the chambers of the Sneferu tombs. This type of construction, typical for Egypt of the period, was probably determined by the fact that the rooms were no longer cut out of the natural rock under the pyramid itself; it was necessary to employ a method that could resist the enormous weight of the limestone blocks above the rooms.

Even a cursory examination of certain technical aspects of the two Dashur pyramids reveals their experimental character. The problems the builders had to solve were not easy; the ones that apparently occupied them most were the slope of the faces of the pyramid and the structure's internal arrangements. It is clear that the architects were searching for the most practical form of construction, and Egyptian geometry at that time tended to resolve problems with fractions and equations as practical as they were simple. The slope of the pyramid faces can be expressed by means of the ratio between the vertical increase and the horizontal. But where the ratio in the Step Pyramid at Sakkara was 7:2 — that is, for every increase of seven units vertically there was an increase of two units horizontally— the ratio for the lower part of the Bent Pyramid was 7:5 and that of the upper part was 14:15. The Red Pyramid has a slope ratio of 14:15 overall. There were still other problems involved, of course, and it is in the framework of their various solutions that we must view the different slopes used in the pyramids of that period.

One other detail about the Dashur pyramids is worth mentioning. The blocks that make up the core of the Bent Pyramid are set in sloping layers, like those in the step pyramids of the Third Dynasty. This is one of several details that once caused scholars to think that the Bent Pyramid belonged to an older period than the Red Pyramid, because this latter has horizontal layers. Such a detail is important in construction. When the layers are sloped so as to remain perpendicular to the outer casing of the pyramid, the blocks used for the facing can be a simple parallelepipidon — that is, each pair of opposite sides are on the same plane. But if the layers of the core remain horizontal, the facing blocks must have their outer sides cut obliquely, according to the inclination of the pyramid. With this latter method, the facing blocks will have a rectangular trapezoid section (as opposed to the simple rectangular section of those pyramids with sloping layers) and this required greater skill and precision in the cutting of the stone.

9. Sakkara: The Pyramid of Unas (Fifth Dynasty) as seen from the east. In the foreground is the end of the sacred way coming from the Temple of the Valley. The two granite doorposts in front of the pyramid mark the entrance to the pyramid temple.

The Pyramids of Giza

Because of their proximity to modern Cairo, their enormous size, and the technical precision with which they were built, the three pyramids at Giza are without a doubt the best known of the ancient Egyptian monuments. The ancient Greeks considered them to be among the Seven Wonders of the World and they remain among the most celebrated monuments of all times. Their fame is fully justified: having once reached the plateau of Giza from which the pyramids have dominated the Nile Valley for some 4500 years, no tourist can remain indifferent.

We have already dealt with the technical questions of how they were constructed, but if we want to consider the Giza pyramids within their epoch and thus understand them better, we must examine the problems that confronted the builders. In this respect, our examination of the preceding royal pyramids should be kept in mind. What we can deduce from the Dashur pyramids, for instance, shows how the ancient architects, having in mind a certain form, tried various approaches in order to realize it in the simplest and fastest way. Above all, they were anxious to ensure the permanence and the inviolability of the monuments.

The greatest effort in this direction was expended in the construction of the Great Pyramid of Cheops at Giza. Its internal arrangement demonstrates that the pyramid was constructed in three successive stages, modified each time. The burial chamber was first cut out of the natural rock under the pyramid; in a second stage it was cut out of

10. Sakkara: The tomb chamber in the Pyramid of Unas, with some of the wall inscriptions that comprise the Pyramid Texts, the most ancient Egyptian texts known.

the pyramid itself; then a third chamber was again cut out of the core of the pyramid, this time at a higher level. The Cheops pyramid is the only pyramid whose burial chamber is entirely cut out of the body of the structure itself. Consequently, the access corridor assumed a singular character; in practical terms, it had to be an ascending corridor. The fact that it was to be sealed off once the pharaoh's funeral had taken place, and that shifting the blocks would be easier if they were moved from a higher level to a lower one, probably induced the builders to store the blocks inside the pyramid during construction. This would explain the great gallery, the last and most famous part of the ascending corridor: the space necessary for storing the blocks was obtained by widening this part and arranging there some support scaffolding for the blocks. A passage was left free to move the dead king's body into the burial chamber; and after the proper rites, the scaffolding was knocked away and the blocks slid down and sealed the access corridor. Widening the corridor, however, posed a problem with the roof, as that space was too wide to be covered with monoliths. They thus used the same system adopted for the Dashur pyramids, corbeling — that is, blocks placed in steadily jutting rows so that the walls met at the top.

This at least partially explains the arrangement of the inner chambers of the Cheops pyramid. Nevertheless, we do not understand all the other factors that lie behind these technical ones. We do not know, for example, why the project was changed twice, nor do we know why they decided to place the burial chamber within the pyramid itself, and not in the rock below. We shall never know. But we must certainly exclude the theory that sees in the arrangement of the chambers, and corridors, and in their measurements, some sort of formula for the entire system of knowledge of the ancient Egyptians — their beliefs, their religious system — or even a prophecy of the entire course of future history, as if the measurements of the pyramid were like a horoscope. However diverting such theories may be (and there are many like them), they are based on two contradictory considerations. First we are asked to accept that the science and technology of the builders of the pyramids was of such a primitive level that a kind of revelation from on high was necessary; then we are to accept the precision with which the Cheops pyramid was realized, as well as an entire series of relationships that can be verified in its measurements and proportions. But such contradictions simply encourage the mystics to elaborate their theories to the limits of absurdity. The only reason we even mention such theories is that they persist in distracting people from the true marvels of the great pyramids.

We have seen that the Egyptians of the Fourth Dynasty had behind them centuries of experience in working with stone that their means of organization was more than equal to the task at hand, and that the proportions of the pyramids were based on a series of relationships that simplified their construction. In the Cheops pyramid, these relationships are so perfectly linked as to suggest "miraculous" correspondences. The slope of its faces, for instance, is at a 14:11 ratio. Not only that, but the ratio of the slope height (a line perpendicular to the base-edge of the faces) to the height of the pyramid is equal to the ratio of the pyramid's height to the semi-median (a horizontal line midway up the pyramid face): this means, for the geometry-lover, a "golden section" relationship. One could proceed in this way to demonstrate how accurately each little part of the pyramid was cal-

11. Sakkara: The interior of the chapel of the Mastaba of Ti, a nobleman of the Fifth Dynasty. A false door contains a statue of the tomb occupant; in front of the statue is an offerings table; reliefs representing the deceased are on the walls.

On the following page:
12. Sakkara: A detail from one of the reliefs on the walls of the chapel of the Mastaba of Ti; represented here is a typical scene from daily life — a herdsman leading the cattle to water.

Sakkara: The Mastaba of Ti
1 Entrance
2 Chapels
3 Shaft
4 Subterranean burial chamber

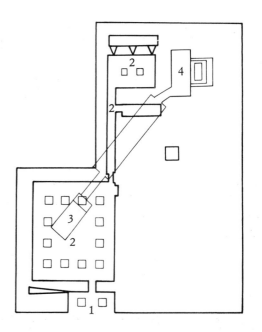

culated. Of course, all this is the very opposite of miraculous; instead, it indicates how methodically the architects established the relationships to reduce construction difficulties.

The Great Pyramid of Cheops also represents the apex of the stone-cutting skill in the Old Kingdom, as well as of the state's capacity to organize the work. We have already seen, in the case of King Djoser's mortuary complex at Sakkara, how by the Third Dynasty the central administration completely controlled the resources of the country. During the course of the Fourth Dynasty, this process evidently developed even further, and the power of the pharaoh became more solidly entrenched. Yet the other two pyramids of Giza, those of Chephren and Mycerinus (again, the Greek versions of Egyptian names, Khafre and Menkaure) built after Cheops' pyramid, do not present any significantly new technical developments. In both cases, however, at least two different projects for construction have left traces of the change in the arrangement of the interior. And the Chephren pyramid, aside from the facing stones remaining around its peak, is historically exceptional because the other structures of its complex are fairly well preserved, thus affording us further invaluable documentation of the Old Kingdom.

The Temples at the Pyramids

We have emphasized that each pyramid was part of an architectural complex composed of various structures. We have also glimpsed — in the case of Djoser's pyramid — some of the ties linking such structures to a highly developed political, religious, and artistic complex that still is not completely understood. In the Fourth Dynasty, at the same time that the step form of the pyramid was giving way to the triangular form, we can also note a change in the architecture and in the general lay-out of the mortuary complex. The most evident novelty is the so-called Valley Temple (up to today, not discovered in any Third Dynasty complex). The pyramids, together with the enclosure that surrounds them, were constructed on the hills that formed the borders of the desert. But during the Fourth Dynasty, a temple was erected where the cultivated land ended and where the waters of the Nile arrived. This Valley Temple was connected to the pyramid enclosure by a sort of "sacred way," which was paved and lined on both sides by limestone walls. At the upper exit of the sacred way, another temple was erected — the so-called pyramid temple — connected directly to the enclosure. Such a pyramid temple existed in the Djoser complex, situated north of the pyramid, whereas in the Fourth Dynasty it was located to the east. What was the function of the pyramid temple? Evidently it was used for the services consecrated to the dead sovereign. And at this point, it would be well to glance at some of the Egyptians' religious beliefs relevant to these structures.

According to a famous myth, the first king of Egypt was a god, Osiris. He had a wife, Isis, and a brother Seth, and governed his people humanely and wisely, teaching them the skills of cultivation, the use of laws, and piety for the gods. But Seth, desiring to usurp the throne of Egypt, killed Osiris, dissected his body, and took his place. Isis fled, but later succeeded in recovering the parts of her husband's body; she then revived him through magic, and in doing so a son was born, Horus. Osiris was no longer able to be king of the living; instead, he became king of the dead, while Horus avenged his father and reconquered the usurped throne.

The implications of the myth are numerous and complicated. What we need to grasp here is its links with Egyptian royalty. In fact, each pharaoh, upon ascending the throne, relived Horus' victory and thus became a "Horus"; whereas every pharaoh that died reenacted the passion of Osiris and was thus an "Osiris." The ancient Egyptians believed that the souls of the dead could live in the next world on one condition: the soul had to have some "support" in this world. This meant that the soul had to have a house, to be fed, and to retain its body. In this context, the tomb was the house, the offerings were the food; the body was both the corpse itself — mummified so that it would last as long as possible — and the various representations of it, such as statues or relief carvings.

The cult of the dead king demanded the daily presentation of offerings, which were deposited before a false door, the communication point between the world of the living and that of the dead. False doors in some pyramid temples indicate that such temples were used basically in the ritual of the presentation of the offerings — that is, for maintaining the king in the hereafter. We can deduce from this that the Valley Temple was the place where the body of the dead king was received, embalmed, and thus "revived," as Isis had done with Osiris. In other words, the Valley Temple was for the funeral ceremony in which the dead king became Osiris.

What should strike our attention here is not only the presence *per se* of the Temple of the Valley but also the absence, in the complexes of the Fourth Dynasty, of structures, symbolic or otherwise, that directly evoked the exclusively political aspects of regality. More to the point, there are no structures that made it possible for the dead pharaoh's soul to continue carrying out his functions. Now the only Valley Temple (actually the only temple of the Old Kingdom) still standing is that of Chephren. If we examine its plan, we immediately note that the design of the interior does not correspond with that of the outside of the temple. While the exterior has a rectangular shape devoid of any decoration, the interior has two basic rooms that form a T shape, with a roof supported by square pillars of pink granite. Here, too, there is no decoration. This is, therefore, the reverse — at least in architectural form — of the Djoser complex, where the structures had a facade but no interior. Also contrary to what we noted at Sakkara, there are no reminders of the earlier stoneless architecture. The surfaces are all smooth, and even the manner of construction is substantially different. No longer are blocks of stone used like bricks, but large blocks are now being used as actual load-bearing elements (like pillars and architraves).

Such a type of construction presupposes remarkable technical skill and, above all, experience in dealing with the material. We can partially explain this architecture by considering that the Egyptians had been steadily perfecting construction techniques since King Djoser's time. Beyond this, the indication of another transformation — that of intent — is to be found in this change of the temple plan. Eliminating everything superficial, reaching a concept of a temple with values and functions completely removed from the purely political aspect of royalty — perhaps all this signified a greater detachment on the part of the king himself. That is to say, if the mortuary complex of the king no longer required even the semblance of the structures in which he

THE BIRTH OF THE THREE CHILDREN

Now on one of these days it came to pass that Red-dedet suffered the pangs of childbirth. Then said the majesty of Re of Sakhebu to Isis, Nephthys, Mesekhent, Heket, and Khnum: "Up, go ye and deliver Red-dedet of the three children that are in her womb, that will exercise this excellent office in this entire land. They will build your temples, they will furnish your altars with victuals, they will replenish your libation tables, and they will make great your offerings." Then these deities went, when they had taken on the forms of dancing-girls, and Khnum was with them and bore their carrying-chair.

And they came to the house of Rewoser and found him standing with loin-cloth hanging down. Then they presented to him their necklaces and rattles. And he said unto them: "My mistresses, behold there is a lady here who is in travail." And they said: "Let us see her; lo, we understand midwifery." And he said unto them: "Come." Then they entered in before Red-dedet, and shut the door of the room upon them and her. And Isis placed herself in front of her, and Nephthys behind her, and Heket hastened the birth. And Isis said: "Be not lusty in her womb as truly as thou art named User-ref." This child slipped forth on to her hands, a child of one cubit with strong bones; the royal titulary of his limbs was of gold, and his head-cloth of true lapis lazuli. They washed him, cut his navel-string, and laid him on a sheet upon a brick. And Mesekhent drew near unto him and she said: "A king that will exercise the kingship in the entire land." And Khnum gave health to his body.

[AESW, pp. 44–5]

THE DEAD KING BECOMES A STAR. FROM A PYRAMID TEXT

This Great One has fallen on his side, he who is in Nedit is felled. Your hand is taken by Re, your head is lifted up by the Two Enneads. Behold, he has come as Orion, behold, Osiris has come as Orion, Lord of Wine in the festival. 'My beautiful one!' said his mother; 'My heir!' said his father of him whom the sky conceived and the dawn-light bore. O King, the sky conceives you with Orion, the dawn-light bears you with Orion. He who lives, lives by the command of the gods, and you live. You will regularly ascend with Orion from the eastern region of the sky, you will regularly descend with Orion into the western region of the sky, your third is Sothis pure of thrones, and it is she who will guide you both on the goodly roads which are in the sky in the Field of Rushes.

[AEPT, pp. 147–8]

carried out his earthly functions, this means that, in a certain sense, he no longer needed them while alive. In turn, this means that his divinity as king was now being taken for granted. Moreover, everything the architects of the Fourth Dynasty did hints at a tendency to express only what was strictly necessary (as shown, for example, by the scarcity of inscriptions — in the case of the dynasty's pyramids, non-existent). In essence, the divinity of the Fourth Dynasty pharaohs was even more solidly established than during the preceding dynasty.

The Mastabas of the Functionaries

Obviously the king, however much deified, could not govern the country alone; that is, he needed subordinates and structures to guarantee the life of the state. Therefore a class of administrators was created, high ministers and state functionaries through whom the king could exercise his power. We know many of these high functionaries quite well; in fact, we might say that most of what we know about the Old Kingdom is due to them. The mummies, rock tombs, mortuary drawings, and relief carvings — all of which evokes the memory of ancient Egypt — when they did not belong to pharaohs, belonged to this class of administrative officials. This is consistent with our earlier observation that what has survived of ancient Egypt almost exclusively reflects its dominating class.

Thousands of Egyptian tombs, some even older than the pyramids, have been found, but the great majority of the population knew only the simplest type of tomb consisting of a pit dug out of the desert sand into which the corpse was placed. The pit was then refilled with sand, and probably marked only by a mound of sand, or by simple mud-brick structures, near which the offerings were placed. But even such crude tombs relate to the ancient Egyptians' belief, already discussed, that the soul needed some earthly support in order to survive. It follows then that the more ambitious the structure, the more possibility the soul has of surviving. It also makes sense that the size and complexity of the tomb should be proportionate to the wealth and social importance of its owner. Therefore, in the Old Kingdom the functionaries' tombs follow those of the pharaohs in order of importance. These tombs are called "mastabas" because their form resembles the mud benches (in Arabic, *mastabah*) that still may be seen outside Egyptian houses.

Basically, a functionary's tomb consisted of a shaft cut out of the natural rock, at the bottom of which was a room containing the sarcophagus with the corpse. At the shaft-opening on the surface was the mastaba proper, a rectangular brick superstructure, its outer walls covered with a smooth limestone casing and inclining slightly toward the center. Functionaries' tombs varied considerably in size, proportion, and technical construction, but the mastaba form had the special function of serving as the place of worship of the dead.

For the pharaohs, the complex of mortuary structures was extremely complicated, since the deification of the king presupposed a series of religious observances. With private persons, this was not the case. If the king, a god on earth, did not have to account to anyone for his behavior, the functionary had many obligations. Named by the king, one might say "created" by the king, he had to answer for his acts to the king; moreover it was the king who granted him the privilege

On the following pages:
13. Sakkara: Detail of the chapel reliefs in the Mastaba of Ti. From a boat made of woven papyrus, two hunters are about to spear hippopotamuses. Note, at the bottom left, the rear part of a crocodile with the sculptor's correction of the design of the leg. To the right are the papyrus stalks, from which frogs and over-sized locusts watch the hunting scene.

of having a special tomb. It was thus the official's job to demonstrate that he merited such a privilege. This means that the possibility of survival of his soul was closely connected to the way he carried out the duties given to him by the king.

But allowing for such differences, the function of the mastaba was somewhat like that of the pyramid. Whereas the temple connected to the pyramid was designed for offerings to the king, private persons had a chapel on the east side of the mastaba. This chapel is of great interest. Originally it consisted of a mere niche cut out of the wall that was closed by a false door, a stone representation of a door that symbolized the link between the land of the living and that of the dead; the offerings were laid in front of the false door. One can see how such an area became the crucial element of the entire superstructure. The niche-chapel was the part of the tomb most subject to change, since the survival of the dead man's soul depended on it, and since it was, in a sense, the focal point. And, indeed, it was not long before a wall parallel to the eastern facade of the mastaba was built; this defined a long, narrow space that served as the gathering place for the presentation of the offerings. With the addition of further corridors and rooms,

14. Sakkara: Detail from the chapel reliefs of the Mastaba of Ti. Standing on a papyrus boat, Ti himself watches the hippopotamus hunt taking place in the reeds.

15. Sakkara: A detail from the chapel reliefs of the Mastaba of Ti. The women represent personifications of the domains under Ti's supervision, and they are here bringing forth the produce of the land.

A DECREE OF TEMPLE PRIVILEGE, FROM A FIFTH DYNASTY PHARAOH

I

I do not permit that any man have the right to — take away any prophets who are in the District in which thou art, for the corvée, as well as any other work of the District, except to do service for the god himself in the temple in which he is and to conserve the temples in which they are. They are exempt in the length of eternity by the decree of the King of Upper and Lower Egypt: Nefer-iri-ka-Re. There is no title to them in any other service.

II

I do not permit that any man have the right to carry off *the necessary* equipment for any work to any other God's Field on which there is priestly service by any prophets. They are exempt in the length of eternity by the decree of the King of Upper and Lower Egypt: Nefer-iri-ka-Re. There is no title to them in any service.

III

I do not permit that any man have the right to take away any serfs who are on any God's Field on which there is priestly service by any prophets, for the corvée, as well as any other work of the District. They are exempt in the length of eternity by the decree of the King of Upper and Lower Egypt: Nefer-iri-ka-Re. There is no title to them in any service.

[ANET, p. 212]

which penetrated deeper into the interior of the superstructure, there developed the most complex type of mastaba built toward the end of the Old Kingdom. And the larger the network, the greater the wall area to be painted or sculpted, and thus the greater the possibility of survival in the hereafter.

Let us recall that, for the ancient Egyptian, representing objects or persons meant in a certain sense evoking them, making them live again. With this concept in mind, we can deduce that the Egyptian artistic representations did not aim so much at reproducing actual reality as at describing what that reality *should* be, at least in the artist's mind. If, therefore, a state functionary wanted to have himself represented in the exercise of his duties, the artist would describe, almost narrate, what these duties were *ideally* and how diligently they had been fulfilled — especially since the representations would serve as a model for eternity, and would therefore constitute a kind of report of the functionary's activities on earth.

The oldest mastabas go back to the Fourth Dynasty (an age in which the functionary class assumed growing importance) and often contain statues of the deceased and his family. But the functionaries

16. Sakkara: Another detail (left) from the chapel reliefs of the Mastaba of Ti shows men bearing offerings.

17. Aswan: The rock tomb of Sebekhotep. On the pillars are paintings of the deceased and his relatives bearing offerings. In the background is a false door, in front of which is the shaft that leads down into the tomb chamber (right).

A PURIFICATION TEXT CONNECTING THE FLOOD WITH OSIRIS. FROM A PYRAMID TEXT

The canals are filled, the waterways are flooded by means of the purification which issued from Osiris. O you priest, you patrician, you ten great ones of the Palace, you ten great ones of On, you Great Ennead, sit down and see the purification of my father this King as one purified with semen and with natron, the saliva which issued from the mouth of Horus, the spittle which issued from the mouth of Seth, wherewith Horus is purified, wherewith the evil which was on him, which Seth did against him, is cast out on the ground; wherewith Seth is purified, and the evil which was on him, which Horus did against him, is cast out on the ground; wherewith this King is purified, and the evil which was on him is cast out on the ground, being what was done against you in company with your spirits.

[AEPT, p. 151]

A THEOLOGICAL TEXT FROM MEMPHIS

Thus all the gods were formed and his Ennead was completed. Indeed, all the divine order really came into being through what the heart thought and the tongue commanded. Thus the *ka*-spirits were made and the spirits were appointed, they who make all provisions and all nourishment, by this speech. Thus justice was given to him who does what is liked, and injustice to him who does what is disliked. Thus life was given to him who has peace and death was given to him who has sin. Thus were made all work and all crafts, the action of the arms, the movement of the legs, and the activity of every member, in conformance with this command which the heart thought, which came forth through the tongue, and which gives value to everything.

Thus it happened that it was said of Ptah: "He who made all and brought the gods into being." He is indeed Ta-tenen, who brought forth the gods, for everything came forth from him, nourishment and provisions, the offerings of the gods, and every good thing. Thus it was discovered and understood that his strength is greater than that of the other gods. And so Ptah was satisfied, after he had made everything, as well as all the divine order. He had formed the gods, he had made cities, he had founded nomes, he had put the gods in their shrines, he had established their offerings, he had founded their shrines, he had made their bodies like that with which their hearts were satisfied. So the gods entered into their bodies of every kind of wood, of every kind of stone, of every kind of clay, or anything which might grow upon him, in which they had taken form. So all the gods, as well as their *ka*'s gathered themselves to him, content and associated with the Lord of the Two Lands.

[ANET, p. 5]

of the Fifth Dynasty produced the great mastabas, the most famous of which is the mastaba of Ti at Sakkara. In these, the original niche-chapel became the hub of an entire network of rooms and corridors whose walls are completely covered with carved reliefs representing the so-called "scenes of daily life." For us today, such reliefs on the mastaba walls are an invaluable source of information about certain details in the daily life of the ancient Egyptians.

Before examining the social and historical aspects of the wall reliefs, it would be well to clarify one point. During the Old Kingdom, at least through the Fifth Dynasty, the most important administrative functionaries were closely bound to the court. Moreover, the possibility of building a worthy tomb and of receiving daily offerings were granted as a privilege to functionaries by the king himself. This suggests that the construction and decoration of the tombs, and certainly the expense of the daily offerings, were assumed by the state. This system profoundly changed the relationships among the king, nobles, and functionary class in general, and also the priests. The king ordered the priests to take care of all the religious observances connected with

the offerings. Besides causing an increase in the temple staff, this had further striking consequences because the clergy obtained the offerings through the cultivation of land given to the temples by the state (that is, by the king) and this land was not taxed.

At the outset, this system worked well to create an equilibrium among the king, the officials, and the clergy, in that the needs and aspirations of each counterbalanced those of the others. However, as the centralized state developed and grew in importance, the duties and jobs connected with it also increased; hence the number of functionaries and the amount of land assigned to the temples grew as well. Gradually the officials began to feel less and less bound to the court. More and more they nurtured their personal ambitions. The clergy also saw its influence steadily growing. Eventually these conflicting interests began to erode the central authority, and after such vast and unproductive operations as the construction of the great Fourth Dynasty pryamids, pharaohs found it harder to control the very forces they had created.

It is no coincidence, then, that the Fifth Dynasty was typified by

18. Aswan: A detail of a relief in the chapel of the tomb of Sebekhotep; it represents the relatives of the deceased bearing offerings.

the construction of large mastabas and small pyramids. The royal sepulchers, on the other hand, decreased in size, and they were no longer constructed in large square limestone blocks, but in smaller, barely polished ones. But even more important were the sun temples located near the royal pyramids, so typical of the Fifth Dynasty. From what archaeologists have been able to reconstruct, these temples were distinguished by an immense obelisk rather squat in form, made of masonry and placed in the center of the courtyard; worship took place around these obelisks. Little more can be said about their physical characteristics, because of their poor state of preservation, but if we consider other facts, these sun temples become more meaningful.

A new title had by this time been introduced in the royal protocol — "Son of Re" — and this was to remain an essential part of the pharaoh's name. Re was the god of the sun whose chief cult center was Heliopolis, situated on the east bank of the Nile a little north of Memphis. "Son of Re" did not identify the figure of the king with a god, but rather placed him in a dependent position, much like a son's relationship with his father. This reflects the decline of the pharaoh's divine stature, as well as his diminished power. And to the extent that the sun temples the pharaohs were now building were modeled after the principal one at Heliopolis, this coincides with the rise of the priesthood of Re.

Another decisive development in the Fifth Dynasty was the inscription on the walls of the inner chambers of the pyramids. These texts were based on the magical-religious formulas used for the deification of the king in the afterlife and have become known as the "Pyramid Texts." The language of these texts is archaic, and probably there was a long oral tradition behind them. Such formulas were sung or chanted at the funeral rites of the king. They represent the most valuable collection of material on ancient Egyptian religion, particularly of the earliest times. Although their language is often difficult to understand (and sometimes incomprehensible), we can detect the tendency to reconcile two different interpretations of the king's destiny in the afterlife. One connected him to the myth of Osiris, the other to Re; neither interpretation dominated, but it is interesting to notice, at this stage of Egyptian history, such an attempt at systematic theology.

EXPEDITIONS DESCRIBED IN THE AUTOBIOGRAPHY OF UNI

His majesty sent me to Ibhet, to bring the sarcophagus, "Chest-of-the-Living," together with its lid and the costly, splendid pyramidion for the pyramid called: "Mernere-Shines-and-is-Beautiful," of the queen.

His majesty sent me to Elephantine to bring a false door of granite, together with its offering-tablet, doors and settings of granite; to bring doorways and offering-tablets of granite, belonging to the upper chamber of the pyramid called: "Mernere-Shines-and-is-Beautiful," of the queen. Then I sailed down-stream to the pyramid called: "Mernere-Shines-and-is-Beautiful," with 6 cargo-boats, 3 tow-boats and only one warship. Never had Ibhet and Elephantine been visited in the time of any kings with only one warship. Whatsoever his majesty commanded me I carried out completely according to all that his majesty commanded me.

His majesty sent me to Hatnub to bring a huge offering-table of hard stone of Hatnub. I brought down this offering-table for him in only 17 days, it having been quarried in Hatnub, and I had it proceed down-stream in this cargo-boat. I hewed for him a cargo-boat of acacia wood of 60 cubits in its length, and 30 cubits in its breadth, built in only 17 days, in the third month of the third season. Although there was no water, I landed in safety at the pyramid called: "Mernere-Shines-and-is-Beautiful;" and the whole was carried out by my hand, according to the mandate which the majesty of my lord had commanded me.

[ARE, I, pp. 148–50]

It is also interesting to observe the desire to write texts in monuments that traditionally had no inscriptions, at least not in their interiors. Here we note a clear need to find further support for a concept — the divinity of the king — that earlier dynasties had taken for granted.

The Nomarchs

The last great pharaoh of the Old Kingdom was the Sixth Dynasty king, Pepy Nakht. But although he instigated various enterprises — including the construction of his own ambitious tomb near Aswan — his reign (some ninety years, or most of the twenty-third century B.C.) marked the beginning of the breakdown of the central authority. By the end of the Old Kingdom — approximately 2200 B.C. — the balance of powers among the king, the clergy, and the functionary class had deteriorated, and the principal loser was the pharaoh. We have observed this in the growth of the Heliopolis priesthood, and in the mastabas which mirrored the process of gradual weakening of the pharaonic power. Now the mastabas were typical of Memphis; it was the tomb of those who lived and worked in the capital and who could boast of high posts linked with the court. However much these functionaries' claims and demands may have grown, they were still bound to certain largely formal obligations that were nevertheless determined by and dependent upon their proximity to the king.

It was at this stage that the provinces made their presence felt for the first time in Egyptian history. The system of government established during the Old Kingdom had virtually ignored them. In the centralization of power, everything comes from on high, and most of Egyptian culture during the Old Kingdom was linked with a certain social class, the nobles and officials. In art, for instance, figurative representation was extraordinarily uniform throughout Egypt during that period; there did not exist different "schools," varying styles, or local productions.

And yet the provinces existed. Egypt was administratively subdivided into various districts, or provinces (now known by the Greek name, nome), each of which had a governor (the nomarch). No sooner did the central power begin to show signs of weakening than these nomarchs began to express their personal ambitions and aspirations. They did so in what was, for them, the most obvious way (even if this may seem strange to us): they simply prepared tombs for themselves that are remarkable for their size, their network of rooms and corridors, and the solutions to their architectural problems. These tombs were constructed near the capital of their nomes — at Elephantine, Assiut, Beni Hasan, and Thebes, to mention only the most celebrated or best preserved complexes. And so there grew up cemeteries with varying styles and traditions, even if all these tended to be influenced by the basic style established at Memphis.

Since we know by now how much was expressed by the tombs of the ancient Egyptians, this development can not be underestimated. With the weakening of the central power a tendency developed to make administrative posts hereditary. This encouraged independent aspirations which were soon expressed in forms other than tombs with decorated walls. Some of the nomarchs even demonstrated their political ability and eventually played a decisive role in the country's destiny. When this happened, the Old Kingdom of the first pharaohs came to an end and Egypt entered a century of disorder, now known as the First Intermediate Period.

MORTUARY TEMPLE CONTRACT OF HEPZEFI

Contract which the count, the superior prophet, Hepzefi, triumphant, made with the lay priests of Upwawet, lord of Siut, to wit: There shall be given to him:

A white loaf per each individual among them, for his statue, which is in the temple, in the first month of the first season, on the eighteenth day, the day of the Wag-feast.

And they shall go forth, following his mortuary priest, at his glorification, when the fire is kindled for him, as they do when they glorify their own noble ones, on the day of kindling the fire in the temple. Now, this white bread shall be under the charge of my mortuary priest.

He hath given to them for it:

Fuel for every bull, and fuel for every goat, which they give into the storehouse of the count, when each bull and each goat is offered to the temple, as ancient dues which they give into the storehouse of the count. Lo, he hath remitted it to them, not collecting it from them.

And hath given to them 22 jars of beer and 2,200 flat loaves which the official body of the temple give to him in the first month of the first season, on the eighteenth day, as compensation, for their giving white bread per each individual among them, from that which is due to them from the temple, and as compensation for his glorification.

Lo, he spake to them, saying: "If this fuel be reckoned against you by a future count; behold, this bread and beer shall not be diminished, which the official body of the temple deliver to me, which I have given to you. Behold, I have secured it by contract from them."

Lo, they were satisfied with it.

[ARE, I, pp. 163–5]

THE INSTRUCTION OF PRINCE HORDEDEF, SON OF CHEOPS

Beginning of the instruction which the Hereditary Prince and Count, the King's Son Hordedef, made for his son, . . .

Be not boastful before my very eyes, and beware of the boasting of another. If thou art a man of standing and foundest a household, take thou a wife as a man of feeling, and a male child will be born to thee.

Thou shouldst build thy house for thy son in the place where thou art. Embellish thy house of the necropolis, and enrich thy place of the West. A lowly reception is for him who is dead, but a high reception for him who is living, and thy house of death is destined for life.

[ANET, p. 419]

THE MIDDLE KINGDOM

The Reestablishment of Pharaonic Power

With the reunification of Egypt by the Eleventh Dynasty kings, a century of disorder came to an end and the Middle Kingdom period is considered to have begun. One often reads something to the effect that "the Egyptian soul found its typical expression in the dimension of the colossal," but whoever would hold to such an image of the Egyptian world must ignore the Middle Kingdom — one of the most characteristic periods of pharaonic civilization. For one thing, the Middle Kingdom produced no grandiose architectural constructions such as the pyramids of Giza or the Hypostyle Hall at Karnak (which was erected in the New Kingdom). And in general we know this period better through other sources of information than through its architectural monuments.

There are several reasons why, the first and most important being that they were largely destroyed. Then, too, the kings of this epoch — in particular, those of the Twelfth Dynasty, the most representative of the Middle Kingdom — pursued a different policy in their relations with the various forces in the country and, in so doing, did not inspire the construction of temples and other fine buildings. For that matter, even the Old Kingdom is known to us primarily through its tombs; of all its temples, which must have existed in great numbers all over the country, only one survived relatively intact — the Valley Temple of Chephren, which we have described earlier.

We need not explain again why mainly the tombs and temples, and not the centers of habitation, have survived from Egyptian civilization. The Middle Kingdom shares the same fate as the Old Kingdom in this respect. But another element should be noted. Royal tombs of the Middle Kingdom have been preserved, but they are not as revealing of their time as were those of the preceding period — or perhaps it is more accurate to say that they enlighten us in a more indirect way. As for the temples, if those of the Old Kingdom were badly preserved, those of the Middle Kingdom are all but unknown. (Among the few exceptions are the sanctuary of Amon that King Sesostris I built — illustrated here — and the Temple of Mentuhotep I at Deir el-Bahri — to be discussed in detail when we explore that site in the New Kingdom.) This is because the succeeding period, the New Kingdom (in particular, the Eighteenth and Nineteenth Dynasties), was one of intense building activity, and very often older structures were profoundly changed, incorporated into the new buildings or even demolished. (It is impossible today to reconstruct even the most basic structures of the Middle Kingdom.) Behind that statement, however, lies the seeming contradiction that the New Kingdom continued to draw on the experience of the Middle Kingdom — much more so than either looked to the Old Kingdom. This created a situation whereby the cultures of the two periods often seemed to merge; or

20. Cairo, The Egyptian Museum: A statue of King Mentuhotep III (Eleventh Dynasty), made of painted sandstone. The statue was originally in the mortuary temple of the king at Deir el-Bahri (West Thebes). Each of the details signified something to the ancient Egyptians: the red crown was a symbol of Lower Egypt, the beard with the curled end was typical of the gods, the black skin was associated with the god Osiris, and the white garment was the one worn by sovereigns during "jubilee" celebrations.

put in other terms, the pharaohs of the New Kingdom often moved in the same direction, and acted in the same way, as those of the Twelfth Dynasty. We see this tendency expressed in the maintenance and development of the old monuments and places of worship, so that the "demolition" and transformation of older temples was not a rejection of the past, but rather a desire to enter more deeply into the experiences of that past.

The pharaoh of the Middle Kingdom is much more akin to the New Kingdom than to the Old Kingdom sovereign. This is understandable if only because of their proximity in time. Beyond that, the pharaohs of the Middle and New Kingdoms faced much the same general problems in the organization of power. But this still leaves the question: In what historic-political situation did the Middle Kingdom pharaoh develop? The Eleventh Dynasty kings who founded the Middle Kingdom, the Mentuhoteps, in their successful attempt to strengthen the central power that could support an effective royal presence in the country, had to begin from a substantially different political basis than that of the Old Kingdom.

In order to govern, the king now needed functionaries and nomarchs — representatives of the very groups that in the preceding period had split Egypt into autonomous areas, or principalities (as opposed to nomes, the pharaohs' administrative subdivisions). As far as we can deduce, the Mentuhoteps met the challenge by taking advantage of the inevitable conflicts that arose between one principality and the other. The Middle Kingdom pharaohs' final victory must have been essentially military.

Once the rival principalities were defeated and the nation was unified through military force, the Mentuhoteps were far from having completely resolved the situation. They had only simplified it to their own disadvantage; that is, they had organized a state without having eliminated the central forces. This last and most important aspect of the problem could be resolved only by strengthening the royal power while defining quite rigorously the jurisdiction of each nomarch. The pharaohs, however, had to take care not to allow the local powers direct access to the government. The whole state apparatus had to be reviewed and brought up-to-date on this new basis.

The Twelfth Dynasty's Solutions

It was the Twelfth Dynasty that took on this task and successfully concluded it. Its founder, Amenemes I, was not a prince by blood: this fact alone is an obvious indication of the new political situation. In such a difficult situation, he had two factors working against him when it came to restoring the pharaoh-as-god concept. First, the

THE CONDITION OF EGYPT AT THE END OF THE OLD KINGDOM. FROM THE LAMENT OF IPUWER

Door keepers say: "Let us go and plunder." . . . The laundryman refuses to carry his load. . . . Birdcatchers have marshaled the battle array. . . . Men of the Delta marshes carry shields. . . . A man regards his son as his enemy. . . . A man of character goes in mourning because of what has happened in the land. . .

Why really, the face is pale. The bowman is ready. Robbery is everywhere. There is no man of yesterday. . . .

Why really, the Nile is in flood, but no one plows for himself, because every man says: "We do not know what may happen throughout the land!"

Why really, women are dried up, and none can conceive. Khnum cannot fashion mortals because of the state of the land.

Why really, poor men have become the possessors of treasures. He who could not make himself a pair of sandals is now the possessor of riches. . . .

Why really, many dead are buried in the river. The stream is a tomb, and the embalming place has really become the stream.

Why really, nobles are in lamentation, while poor men have joy. Every town says: "Let us banish many from us."

Why really, . . . dirt is throughout the land. There are really none whose clothes are white in these times.

Why really, the land spins around as a potter's wheel does. The robber is now the possessor of riches. . . .

Why really, the River is blood. If one drinks of it, one rejects it as human and thirsts for water.

Why really, doors, columns, and floor planks are burned up, but the flooring of the palace — life, prosperity, health! — still remains firm. . . .

Why really, crocodiles sink down because of what they have carried off, for men go to them of their own accord. . . .

Why really, the desert is spread throughout the land. The nomes are destroyed. Barbarians from outside have come to Egypt. . . . There are really no people anywhere. . . .

Why really, they who built pyramids have become farmers. They who were in the ship of the god are charged with forced labor. No one really sails north to Byblos today. What shall we do for cedar for our mummies? Priests were buried *with* their produce, and nobles were embalmed with the oil thereof as far away as Keftiu, but they come no longer. Gold is lacking. . . . How important it now seems when the oasis-people come carrying their festival provisions: reed-mats, . . . fresh plants, . . . birds, and. . .

Why really, Elephantine, the Thinite nome, and the shrine of Upper Egypt do not pay taxes because of civil war. . . . What is a treasury without its revenues for? The heart of the king must indeed be glad when truth comes to him! But really, every foreign country comes! Such is our water! Such is our welfare! What can we do about it? Going to ruin!

Why really, laughter has disappeared, and is no longer made. It is wailing that pervades the land, mixed with lamentation. . . .

doctrine had been discredited by the relatively recent disintegration of the Old Kingdom; and second, as mentioned, Amenemes himself was not of royal blood. Thus arose the policy of the first part of the dynasty, the effort to establish the absolute and undisputed supremacy — more especially, its divine stamp — of the king over all other mortals. The nomarchs were allowed a certain autonomy, but within the framework of the newly reorganized royal policy. They were given, for example, the right to conscript troops to be used for certain public works and other obligatory jobs. At the same time, the king understood quite well that, in order to avoid the same fate that befell the royal power in the Old Kingdom, it was necessary to keep the nomarchs in continuous agitation. This is what prompted the king's frequent visits to the provinces: the local powers would never get the impression that the pharaoh was unaware of their existence.

Moreover, the pharaohs launched a series of military expeditions outside the traditional geographic confines of Egypt; the first went into Nubia, the area that extends southward from the first cataract of the Nile. The Nubian expeditions are of primary importance in the history of Egyptian royalty, for several reasons. First of all, there was gold in Nubia, which meant a sizable enrichment of the royal treasury allowing the pharaoh greater independence to combat antagonistic national elements. In the second place, such expeditions served as a fine excuse to employ those troops conscripted by the provincial governors. This drained some of the energy from local politics and exhausted the nomarchs' labor force, so essential for the accumulation of goods which was essential for any potential "political base." Moreover, this labor force came to be tightly bound to the central state, which probably financed the expeditions and maintained the troops. Thus there was created, even though indirectly, a new relationship

21. Karnak: The sanctuary of Amon, a chapel dedicated by King Sesostris I (Twelfth Dynasty) and to be used as a resting place for Amon's sacred boat during the course of processions in the god's honor. Found as the filling for the third pylon of the Temple of Amon at Karnak, the chapel has been reconstructed in the temple enclosure.

FROM THE LAMENT OF IPUWER

Why really, the children of nobles are dashed against the walls. The once prayed-for children are now laid out on the high ground. . . .

Why really, the entire Delta marshland will no longer be hidden: the confidence of the Northland is now a beaten path. What is it that one could do?. . . Behold, it is in the hands of those who did not know it, as well as those who knew it; foreigners are now skilled *in* the work of the Delta. . . .

Why really, all maid-servants make free with their tongues. When their mistresses speak, it is burdensome to the servants. . . .

Why really, the ways *are not* guarded roads. Men sit in the bushes until the benighted traveler comes, to take away his burden and steal *what is* on him. He is presented with the blows of a stick and slain wrongfully. . . . Ah, would that it were the end of men, no conception, no birth! Then the earth would cease from noise, without wrangling! . . .

Why really, grain has perished on every side . . . . Everybody says: "There is nothing!" The storehouse is stripped bare; its keeper is stretched out on the ground. . . . Ah, would that I had raised my voice at that time — it might save me from the suffering in which I am!

[ANET, pp. 441–2]

22. Cairo, The Egyptian Museum: Fragment of a pillar from a Karnak chapel dedicated to King Sesostris I. The god Horus, with a falcon's head, embraces the king, who wears the double crown (of Upper and Lower Egypt) and holds a mace in his left hand and a scepter in his right.

THE INSTRUCTIONS FOR KAGEMNI

If thou sittest with many persons, hold the food in abhorrence, even if thou desirest it; it taketh only a brief moment to master oneself, and it is disgraceful to be greedy. . . . A cup of water quencheth the thirst, and if the mouth be full, it strengtheneth the heart. A good thing taketh the place of that which is good, just a little taketh the place of much. He is a miserable man that is greedy for his body. . . .

If thou sittest with a greedy person, eat thou only when his meal is over, and if thou sittest with a drunkard, take thou only when his desire is satisfied. Rage not against the meat; take when he giveth thee, and refuse it not. Think, that softeneth him.

Be not boastful of thy strength in the midst of those of thine own age. Be on thy guard against any withstanding thee. One knoweth not what may chance, what God doeth when He punisheth.

The vizier had his children called after he had completed his treatise on the ways of mankind and on their character as encountered by him. And he said unto them: "All that is in this book, hear it as if I spake it." Then they placed themselves upon their bellies. They read it as it stood in writing, and it was better in their heart than everything that was in this entire land; they stood and they sat in accordance therewith.

The majesty of King Huni came to port, and the majesty of King Snefru was raised up as beneficent king in this whole land. Then was Kagemni appointed superintendent of the capital and vizier.

[AESW, pp. 66-7]

THE INSTRUCTIONS OF THE VIZIER PTAH-HOTEP

Let not thy heart be puffed-up because of thy knowledge; be not confident because thou art a wise man. Take counsel with the ignorant as well as the wise. The full limits of skill cannot be attained, and there is no skilled man equipped to his full advantage. Good speech is more hidden than the emerald, but it may be found with maidservants at the grindstones. . . .

If thou art a leader commanding the affairs of the multitude, seek out for thyself every beneficial deed, until it may be that thy own affairs are without wrong. Justice is great, and its appropriateness is lasting; it has not been disturbed since the time of him who made it, whereas there is punishment for him who passes over its laws. It is the right path before him who knows nothing. Wrongdoing has never brought its undertaking into port. It may be that it is fraud that gains riches, but the strength of justice is that it lasts, and a man may say: "It is the property of my father."

[ANET, p. 412]

between sovereign and subjects, one which had little need of the nomarchs as intermediaries. Yet formally, these governors could not make any objections to the new state of affairs.

The kings of the Twelfth Dynasty were highly calculating of their every act. As proof, we can cite the custom that, as far as is known, they introduced: every pharaoh now shared his throne with the son destined to succeed him, and placed the command of the troops in this son's hands. Here, too, the intention is clear: besides the guarantees afforded by having his own son at the head of the army, the pharaoh made it possible for his heir to make himself known to the people before ascending the throne. This further confirms the king's insecurity in his relations with the nobles and nomarchs, and that the new military expeditions had considerable significance for Egypt's internal political situation.

The Reclamation of the Fayum

The Fayum is a natural depression that extends along the west of the Nile Valley, starting about sixty-five miles southwest of Cairo. It is fed by the Bahr Yusuf, an affluent of the Nile; as the Fayum is a relatively low area, the waters of the Nile can enter it but cannot flow out again and it is a virtual oasis. (Thus Lake Moeris, or Karun, was

FROM THE AUTOBIOGRAPHY OF KETI, GOVERNOR OF ASSIUT

I brought a gift for this city, in which there were no families of the Northland, nor people of Middle Egypt; making a monument, I substituted a channel of ten cubits. I excavated for it upon the arable land. I equipped a gate for it in the ground of one building. I was liberal as to the monument. I sustained the life of the city, I gave the grain-food and water at midday. I supplied water in the highland district, I made a water supply for this city of Middle Egypt in the mountain, which had not seen water. I secured the borders. I made the elevated land a swamp. I caused the water of the Nile to flood over the ancient landmarks. Every neighbor was supplied with water, and every citizen had Nile water to his heart's desire; I gave waters to his neighbors, and he was content with them.

I was rich in grain. When the land was in need, I maintained the city. I allowed the citizen to carry away for himself grain; and his wife, the widow and her son.

[ARE, I, pp. 188–9]

FROM THE TREATISE OF KETI II TO HIS SON, MERIKARA

Thou sufferest not from the Nile, that it cometh not, and thou hast the products of the Delta.

Behold, I drave in the mooring-post, in the East. The boundary from Hebenu unto the Path-of-Horus is settled with cities and filled with people of the best of the entire land, in order to repel the arms of the Asiatics.

I would fain see a brave man, that equalleth me therein, and that doeth more than I have done.

This is said, moreover, with regard to the barbarian: The wretched Asiatic, evil is the land wherein he is, with bad water, inaccessible by reason of the many trees, and the roads thereof are evil by reason of the mountains. Never dwelleth he in a single place and his feet wander. Since the time of Horus he fighteth and conquereth not, but likewise is he not conquered, and he never announceth the day in fighting, like the supporter of a confederacy.

I caused the Delta to smite the foreigners. I made captive their people, I plundered their cattle. Trouble not thyself concerning him, the Asiatic, he plundereth a lonely settlement but he captureth not a populous city.

Behold, that is the navel of the barbarians. Its walls are made ready for battle, its soldiers are many, subjects are in it. . . .

It counts ten thousand men as citizens, who are clean and without imposts. The great men thereof go since the time of Horus to the Residence. Established are its boundaries....There are many northerners who water it; they have made a dyke as far as Herakliopolis.

If thy boundary towards the Southern Land is in revolt, the foreigners of the North will also begin fighting. Build therefore towns in the Delta. A man's name will not be small through what he hath done, and an inhabited city is not harmed. Build towns. . . . The enemy is glad to see that one is afflicted, out of evil nature. King Akhthoes laid it down in his instruction; "Whoso is quiet toward one that is insolent, he injureth. God attacketh him that is hostile towards the temple."

[AESW, pp. 80–1]

formed — now a salt lake because it has no effluent and loses water only by evaporation.) In ancient times, when the waters of the Nile rose higher than they do today, Bahr Yusuf and the Fayum were completely subject to the whims of the river. This meant that the Fayum tended to be a marshy area, with luxuriant, thick vegetation, a realm of crocodiles.

To our knowledge, the first people to render the Fayum habitable did so under the direction of the kings of the Twelfth Dynasty. The Bahr Yusuf, after flanking the Nile Valley for many miles, bends toward the northeast and crosses a short piece of desert before proceeding on to the Fayum depression. In that final stretch, the Middle Kingdom pharaohs constructed a system of dams that made possible the regulation of the annual flow of the waters, and hence the reclamation of the area. This was so successful that even today the Fayum remains one of the most fertile areas in all Egypt.

The political design behind this operation is implied by the fact that the kings of the Twelfth Dynasty, who came from Thebes in Upper Egypt, established their capital at Lisht, some twenty miles south of Memphis and near the point where the Bahr Yusuf bends to cross the desert. Scholars have recently thrown light on the political meaning of the reclamation of the Fayum and the transfer of the capital. Evidently this was undertaken so as to create a rich agricultural area that had the further advantage of not being tied to any local interest. Consequently the king had at his disposal a kind of reserve of economic

forces that were added to those already attained through the exploitation of the Nubian gold.

After this "escalation" of royal power, it is clear that the central authority was firmly entrenched. The influence of the nomarchs had been cleverly deflected by a most audacious and far-sighted policy, carried out with exceptional awareness and perseverance by that magnificent family of Twelfth Dynasty kings. Counting on his prestige among his people, on a well-controlled, organized, and tested army, and on considerable economic resources, the pharaoh could now cope with any challenge to his authority. And, in fact, toward the middle of the dynasty's reign, peripheral powers began to be limited, and the restoration of the king-as-god doctrine commenced. Obviously this doctrine could not be an exact replica of the image formulated during the Old Kingdom. The figure of the king, by the Middle Kingdom, was politically different, just as he faced a different balance of forces than had Old Kingdom rulers. Thus, the new doctrine had to be more dynamic; it could exhalt the divinity of the king, but now his divinity related to his actions as leader of the government. In short, the pharaoh-as-god had to be in constant touch with his subjects; he was "their" god by virtue of being a sovereign who took care of his country.

So it was that the pharaoh, who had remained silent during the entire Old Kingdom, began to speak. He spoke of himself, of what he did or what he wanted to do, but always in relation to his achievements as "governor" of the nation. There thus grew up a series of literary works that set forth the development of the royal family's policy; these works were gradually transformed so that at the end of the Twelfth Dynasty the sovereign was exalted for his superhuman qualities, even his ability to work miracles. The distrust in his collaborators — evident during the difficult times of the reorganization — was replaced by pride in the work achieved and in the power of the royal figure.

To arrive at such a conclusion seems quite natural. But the difference in the pharaoh's image at the end of the Middle Kingdom found another more surprising expression, a development without precedent since the first unification of the nation by Menes-Narmer. The novelty was the new "public": that is, the pharaoh addressed a new category of persons, the middle class of the population. The king spoke to these subjects; they spoke of him. We must certainly not read into this new development our sense of democracy; this never existed throughout pharaonic history. In reality, the middle class of ancient Egypt entered into the calculations of the government's policy only to the extent that it could be used to further unite the nation against the destructive forces.

In the end, these new relationships were compromised, for the power of the pharaohs once again declined. The Middle Kingdom ended but the mass of Egyptians carried on as ever, awaiting the annual "gift" of the Nile.

THE CONQUEST OF NUBIA. FROM THE SEMNEH STELE, SOUTHERN BOUNDARY OF EGYPT

Live the King of Upper and Lower Egypt, Sesostris III, who is given life, stability, satisfaction forever.

Year 16, third month of the second season, occurred his majesty's making the southern boundary as far as Heh. I have made my boundary beyond that of my fathers; I have increased that which was bequeathed to me. I am a king who speaks and executes; that which my heart conceives is that which comes to pass by my hand; one who is eager to possess, and powerful, not allowing a matter to sleep in his heart, attacking him who attacks, silent in a matter, or answering a matter according to that which is in it; since, if one is silent after attack, it strengthens the heart of the enemy. Valiance is eagerness, cowardice is to slink back; he is truly a craven who is repelled upon his border; since the Nubian hearkens to the mouth; it is answering him which drives him back; when one is eager against him, he turns his back; when one slinks back, he begins to be eager. But they are not a people of might, they are poor and broken in heart. My majesty has seen them; it is not an untruth.

I captured their women, I carried off their subjects, went forth to their wells, smote their bulls; I reaped their grain, and set fire thereto. I swear as my father lives for me, I speak its truth, without a lie therein, coming out of my mouth.

[ARE, I, pp. 295–6]

THE NEW KINGDOM

The Emergence of Thebes

With the last of the Twelfth Dynasty pharaohs, in 178? B.C., Egypt once more split up into several parts, both politically and geographically, and was ruled by a series of rival, and largely incompetent, kings. During the ensuing two centuries, known now as the Second Intermediate Period, one part of the country — including the Delta and down to about two hundred miles south of Memphis — was ruled by the Hyksos, the "foreign chieftains" of immigrants (probably mostly Semites) from Asia. But through it all, one Egyptian regime managed to hold out at the city of Thebes, about four hundred miles upriver from Memphis, and it was a Theban family that finally managed, in the first decades of the sixteenth century B.C., to drive the Hyksos out and to reunite Egypt. In so doing, these Thebans not only founded the Eighteenth Dynasty and launched the New Kingdom, but also established their home city as the capital. If we are to understand the monuments of the New Kingdom, we must first understand Thebes — in particular, how and why it came to be the capital of Egypt.

At the beginning of pharaonic Egypt, Menes-Narmer founded Memphis near the apex of the Delta, symbolizing the union of the Two Lands and corresponded with the birth of an entirely new historical entity. From its modest beginnings, Memphis developed into the Egyptian city with the greatest culture and tradition, connected as it was with the very existence of a unified kingdom. Despite everything that transpired in the centuries that followed, Memphis could never be ignored; it continued to exercise its influence throughout the entire history of pharaonic Egypt. Thus the capital of the Twelfth Dynasty at Lisht in the Fayum — placed there for reasons of political expediency — never attained any symbolic significance, or constituted a true alternative to Memphis.

Such was not the case with Thebes. We know nothing of its origins except that they lay far back in time and that at first the city was located only on the east bank of the Nile. The history of Thebes begins for us in the Middle Kingdom, when a certain Amenemes succeeded in seizing power and secured the throne of Egypt for his family, thus founding the Twelfth Dynasty. Now we have already mentioned that the Twelfth Dynasty moved its capital to Lisht even though Amenemes was from Thebes. However, Mentuhotep, a king of the Eleventh Dynasty — the one that had put an end to the disruptive forces of the First Intermediate Period — came from a place near Thebes, Hermontis. Evidently, Thebes was a center for pro-Mentuhotep and anti-Amenemes factions, and this would be still another reason for the Twelfth Dynasty to base itself in the Fayum.

Yet the evidence suggests that all the rulers of the Twelfth Dynasty were constantly preoccupied with activities in Thebes. Thus, the city of Hermontis worshiped Montu as its patron god, and from whom Mentuhotep derived his name. Thebes traditionally worshipped Amon, a ram-headed fertility god, as its patron deity. In order to stress their origins in Thebes, the sovereigns of the Twelfth Dynasty promoted the cult of Amon. It was no coincidence that Amenemes I kept his own name, which derived from Amon, although it was customary for Egyptian kings to assume a new "god-given" name while ruling. In any case, Thebes thereafter emerged as the religious and cultural center of Egypt: and in the breakdown of central authority that accompanied the Second Intermediate Period, Thebes remained an independent bastion of power.

Little is known about the two centuries between the Middle and New Kingdoms when much of Egypt fell under the control of foreigners. Some were descendants of migrants from the Near East who had long been moving into the Delta, and their chieftains were known as Hyksos. Although this was not a time for building monuments, these new people introduced such things as wheeled vehicles, new weapons, an improved loom, and new musical instruments; for most Egyptians, of course, life went on much as ever.

It is also not known for certain just why the Hyksos occupation spared the Theban domain, which extended along the Nile from Thebes to the first cataract. In any case, Thebes found itself in a difficult situation, since it could not remain self-sufficient for long, closed in as it was by the desert to the east and west and by potentially hostile peoples to the south and north. Survival was the primary motive that drove the Theban princes to struggle against the Hyksos. Nor do we know how the Theban rulers raised the forces necessary for supporting their wars. Perhaps the Hyksos power was not all that great.

The ancient Egyptians, it should be said, always had a tendency to place the blame for their internal troubles on the nomadic populations of the Near East who infiltrated their land, especially the eastern region of the Delta. Nomadic peoples of the Near East certainly made their presence felt in the bordering lands, but it is unlikely that mere shepherd tribes could have attained a political influence to shake the foundations of the Egyptian state unless there were first some internal shakiness to begin with. Thus, every time we find the Delta invaded by nomads and substantially controlled by them, we must look for signs of prior domestic strains. Texts of the First Intermediate Period, for instance, refer to such invasions, but we know that the deterioration was essentially due to the conflicting forces that developed in the Old Kingdom.

The New Kings of Egypt

Even if we consider the Hyksos domination in less gloomy tones than tradition usually paints the period, it is quite natural that the Theban princes, on gaining power, would manipulate the presence of the

Hyksos kings for their own ends — namely, to increase their own prestige at the expense of those in Memphis. This is a common political device — even in our time — but we must be careful when judging such ancient history. If we consider how the fifth-century B.C. Athenians were able to exploit even more inconsequential episodes in order to justify the Persian Wars, we should not be surprised to see how the Theban princes were able to found a dynasty soon after ousting the Hyksos occupiers. The daily bread of political struggles is the ability to take advantage of certain facts and situations in the right place and at the right time.

Be that as it may, when the Theban princes Kamose and his brother Ahmose pushed the foreigners out of Egypt, the struggle became a war of national liberation; its heroes were the Thebans and — by an extension that all Egyptians would have understood — the god Amon, patron of the city. In this sense, we can admire the political astuteness of the Eighteenth Dynasty kings who succeeded the Theban princes; they not only knew how to utilize the creation of an empire as the answer to internal pressures, but were also able to support their ambitious projects with an effective theoretical justification (today known as "propaganda"). A new era began for the nation, and as Thebes was credited with the "recovery" of Egypt, it also became the symbol of the new state.

The New Kingdom, then, was to be totally Theban in all its official cultural manifestations. But when we speak of Theban culture, we should not imagine something rooted in a city as we might think of the culture of Athens, Rome, Florence, or Paris. The city in ancient Egypt was the place where various expressions of power emerged, whether of a religious or an administrative nature. Therefore, the culture of the New Kingdom was the culture of Thebes, but only to the extent that the city was the royal residence and the sanctuary of Amon. Thebes, finally, meant Amon.

Thebes and the Power of Amon

It should also be established that the political power of Thebes was inseparable from the power of Amon. In effect, the city had no independent tradition as the seat of secular political power. The struggle against the Hyksos served as an excellent excuse to establish such a tradition. The official theological justification was afforded by the support of Amon, the god who had already demonstrated his efficacy with the advent of Amenemes I in the Twelfth Dynasty.

The pharaoh who emerged from the war against the Hyksos was a different figure from the previous kings of Egypt, motivated in profoundly new ways. The Hyksos phenomenon had been part of the great movements of populations throughout the eastern Mediterranean during the first half of the second millennium B.C. — essentially the release of new social forces. The role that Egypt played in this situation required that the new pharaoh should also keep "up to date," so to speak. Here, by the way, we see another refutation of the thesis that pharaonic Egypt remained unchanged for thousands of years. Here,

On the following pages:
25. Deir el-Bahri: Queen Hatshepsut's mortuary temple, seen from the northeast. She was an Eighteenth Dynasty sovereign. In the background, to the left, can be seen the mortuary temple of the Eleventh Dynasty king, Mentuhotep III.

too, the choice of Thebes as capital takes on a special significance: it stressed a concept of royal power that was set up along substantially different lines.

For instance, when looking for advisers, the pharaoh now began to favor those individuals who rose from the ranks, those whom he had helped to promote; he would mistrust those who had large economic interests or instruments of pressure at their disposal. It was natural, then, for the king to ally himself with persons of non-aristocratic origins — and we shall be meeting some of them; eventually the importance of these new advisers exceeded the pharaohs' expectations, until at the end of the Eighteenth Dynasty, one of them, Horemheb, even took over the throne of Egypt.

Another new development was that the pharaoh of the New Kingdom had also to become a man of action. In effect, the sovereign became

26. Deir el-Bahri: A detail of the reliefs that decorate the walls of the mortuary temple of Queen Hatshepsut. Represented here is the procession of the sacred boat of the goddess Hathor.

27. **Deir el-Bahri: Detail of one of the capitals of the sanctuary dedicated to the goddess Hathor at Queen Hatshepsut's mortuary temple. The goddess was characteristically represented as having a feminine face with the ears of a cow.**

THE VICTORIES OF TUTHMOSIS III. FROM A STELE AT KARNAK

Saith Amon-Re lord of Karnak: Thou comest to me and exultest, when thou seest my beauty, my son, my protector, Menkheperre, living for ever. I shine forth for love of thee. Mine heart is gladdened by thy beauteous coming to my temple, and mine hands impart protection and life to thy limbs.

How pleasing is the kindliness which thou displayest towards my body; so will I establish thee in my dwelling, and work a wonder for thee.

I give thee might and victory over all the hill countries; I set thy glory and the fear of thee in all the low countries, the terror of thee as far as the four pillars of the sky. I make great the reverence for thee in all bodies, and cause the war-cry of thy majesty to resound among the Nine Peoples of the Bow.

The great ones of all foreign lands are held together in thy fist. I myself stretch out mine hands and tie them for thee. I bind together the Troglodytes by tens of thousands and thousands, the Northerners by hundreds of thousands, as captives.

I cause thy foes to fall beneath thy sandals, so that thou treadest down the rebels; even as I consign to thee the earth in its length and its breadth, and the Westerners and Easterners are under thine authority.

[AESW, pp. 254–5]

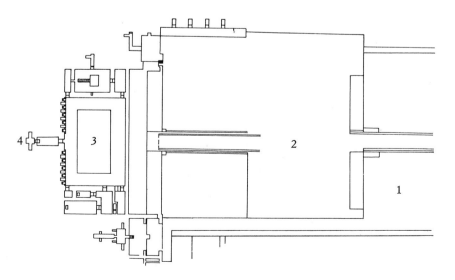

Deir el-Bahri: The Mortuary Temple of Queen Hatshepsut
1 Courtyard
2 First terrace
3 Second terrace
4 Sanctuary

involved in an ever increasing number of military situations, required by the events of the time. A military leader, a commander-in-chief, besides requiring a rapid and agile system of command, must assume heavy responsibilities, on his own and often in haste. The New Kingdom pharaoh thus came to control an army and, by extension, an empire. At the same time, the formation of an empire came to represent an answer to certain internal pressures of Egypt.

The Organization of the New Kingdom

When speaking of the Egyptian empire in the Near East, we should not think of anything similar to the Roman Empire or to the more modern empires or forms of imperialism. Rather, it was a question of control or influence exercised by Egypt on the policies of the city-states and principalities in which the Levant was divided at that time (an area we know today as Syria, Lebanon, Israel, and Jordan). The pharaoh limited himself to establishing military garrisons in the most important centers; these garrisons served as "political observers," while guaranteeing the collection of taxes and tribute. And if Egypt could count on a certain amount of produce (especially wood, so scarce in Egypt) from these small states, they in turn could feel assured of the support of a great power. At the time, money — in our sense of the word — was not used, so that problems connected with monetary circulation did not affect relations between nations or in the internal situation of any single country. Basically, the Egyptian empire was based not so much on force or arms as upon its solid and highly organized administrative structure.

It can be assumed that the organization of the empire required a huge increase in the state's bureaucratic apparatus, forcing it to absorb a great number of administrative personnel. We have already seen how, in the Middle Kingdom, such personnel were no longer recruited from the noble class or from among those closely connected to the court, but more and more drew upon persons from the middle class. Thus, as early as the Middle Kingdom, the government administration relied on a class that took its place between the farmers on the one hand and the rulers on the other. As agents of the central power, these bureaucrats naturally gravitated toward the upper classes and not toward the lower ones. So much so, that they eventually took on the roles that were once strictly limited to the aristocracy. On the other hand, the central authority could not do without these bureaucrats, and gradually enlarged their privileges, so as to keep them tied to the center.

For the farmer, it makes no difference which rulers are gathering the taxes — local sovereigns or foreigners; his condition remains essentially unchanged, and that was the case during the Second Intermediate Period. If, however, the system that controls the resources of the country changes, the state functionaries will see their power limited to a large extent. Inevitably, then, the Egyptian middle class found itself playing an active political role. This development seems to have escaped the notice of the Twelfth Dynasty sovereigns, who felt they were merely using the middle class as a fulcrum to apply pressure against the nomarchs' power. This "politicalization" of the middle class, however, was not a process of democratizing the social structures

28. **Deir el-Bahri: Detail of the reliefs on the walls of the mortuary temple of Queen Hatshepsut. Portrayed here are running soldiers, carrying battle-axes in their right hands and branches in their left hands.**

of ancient Egypt; it is fairer to say that the Egyptian middle class became a sort of political "territory" in the struggle for power.

The first to understand these new social forces, apparently, was Prince Kamose of Thebes, the man who began the revolt against the Hyksos and so helped to pave the way for the New Kingdom. He was credited with writing — in a rather popular style — an account of the expulsion of the Hyksos. Kamose narrates how the nobles advised him to follow a prudent policy, saying that the presence of foreign rulers in the Delta in no way obstructed the Egyptian herds from grazing in their habitual Delta pastures. The nobles had no desire to gamble the certain for the unknown, to embark on a dangerous adventure. The royal power, therefore, aligned itself with the middle class, to create the new pharaohs' political policy.

29. Karnak: The sanctuary of Amon with the two pillars built by Tuthmosis III (Eighteenth Dynasty) in front of the god's sanctuary. The pillars are decorated with heraldic plants symbolizing the Two Lands: the papyrus (rear) as Lower Egypt, the lotus (front) as Upper Egypt.

30. Karnak: This is one of the two obelisks built by Queen Hatshepsut in front of the fifth pylon of the temple of Amon.

31. Karnak: Detail of the reliefs carved on the walls of the temple of Amon. Depicted here is the crucial act of worship: Horus, with a falcon's head (left) and Thoth, with an ibis head (right) pour a stream of the hieroglyphic sign signifying "life," the *ankh* symbol. Note that the figure of the queen, as well as those places in the inscription where her name was written, have been scraped away with a chisel, probably by her successor, Tuthmosis III.

We reject, by the way, the theory that the New Kingdom empire originated in the purely accidental contact with the Asian population, from which there followed a phase of "revenge and reprisal." In the course of this, so the theory goes, the pharaohs, intent on ridding the country of foreign occupation, found themselves, almost without realizing it, chasing the fleeing Asians beyond the border, and then asking themselves with surprise how they got so far from their native land. We must also reject the idea of considering Egyptian history as that of a purely isolationist culture — that is, insulated from and uninterested in the outside world.

At this juncture we can better understand the reasons for the many references to and reminders of the Twelfth Dynasty, apparent in any discussion of the Eighteenth Dynasty. At the same time, it is easier for us to understand the differences between the two periods. Obviously, the organization of the empire necessitated great changes in the country's social structure, giving to the new relationship between king and middle class a permanent stamp it had never had before. This new alignment had consequences for the social structure of the country that probably no one in the Eighteenth Dynasty had been able to

32. Luxor: The temple of Amon, with the colonnaded courtyard, the work of Amenhotep III (Eighteenth Dynasty) seen from the south. To the rear, and center, is Amenhotep III's colonnaded passageway, followed by the colonnaded courtyard of Ramesses II (Nineteenth Dynasty), closed off by a pylon. Note in the central portion the smaller columns, on the same axis as the colonnade; these belong to the chapels of Tuthmosis III (Eighteenth Dynasty) and have been absorbed into the courtyard of Ramesses II. The two minarets in the background (right) are part of a Moslem mosque, constructed on the remains of the ancient pylon.

anticipate. With this in mind, we are now ready to consider the monuments of the New Kingdom — starting with those at Thebes.

The Many Sights of Thebes

The site of the great capital that the ancients knew as Thebes is today the location of the modern Egyptian city of Luxor. Giza is especially familiar because it is so close to Cairo. But visitors to Egypt must make a special effort to get to Luxor; no one just "passes through." However much Luxor is invaded by large modern hotels and tourists from all over the world, it is here that one can still confront the essence of ancient Egypt — that almost organic relationship between man's works and natural features that was Thebes.

As with the other cities of ancient Egypt, only the remains of temples and tombs offer testimony to what Thebes once was, yet their numbers and proportions have made it one of the most imposing archaeological complexes in the world. There are several reasons why so much of ancient Thebes has survived. The Eighteenth Dynasty kings established

33. Luxor: The colonnade of Amenhotep III at the temple of Amon. At the end follows the courtyard of Ramesses II, then the chapels of Tuthmosis III, and the pylon of Ramesses II.

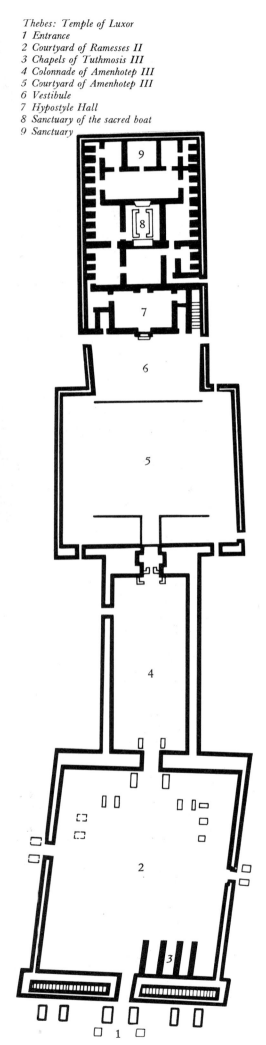

their residence and capital there, thus assuring that the city became the governing force in official Egyptian political life and culture for many centuries to come. As such, it could command all the resources necessary for building and maintaining ambitious architectural projects. And because the royal house adopted the protective rays of Amon, patron deity of Thebes, the monuments were guaranteed the respect due to religious symbols. One final reason for the impressive monuments still to be seen at Thebes is that the city did not share the fate of Memphis, which was virtually dismantled over the centuries. After the Greek, Roman, and Arab conquests, Thebes remained relatively remote from Lower Egypt and the busy world that eventually gravitated around the Mediterranean Sea.

The east bank of the Nile that sustains Luxor is like a vast plain that, when not inundated by the annual floods, is one of the sweetest spectacles Egypt has to offer, with green fields extending for miles and miles. But if you lift your eyes to the west, you see the profound contrast nature is capable of. Unlike the area around Memphis, where the light yellow desert softly descends toward the valley, the desert's presence here is stark and menacing. Rugged hills with tortuous, steep

34. Luxor: The western side of the portico that encloses the courtyard of Amenhotep III in the temple of Amon.

sides, dominate the entire river valley. Here is one of the most desolate of spectacles Egypt has to offer. At noon, in the ravines that cut through the hills in every direction, the sun is implacable, the silence profound and almost haunting, and there is not the slightest trace of life. Yet the very hostility of this environment helped to conserve such extremely delicate materials as papyrus and other organic substances in the ancient monuments built — often literally dug out — of the rocky hills on this side of the Nile.

Egyptologists distinguish between West Thebes on the western bank of the Nile, from the original city on the east bank. We have seen how the barren lands flanking the Nile had long been used as burial sites. This was the location of the great tombs of Memphis. We do not know if the Memphite cemeteries — except for the priests who carried out the temple ceremonies — formed the basis of an independent society. Yet this was the case with Thebes. There is a strong possibility that during the late Ptolemaic period this city was even administratively independent from the "city of Amon," the eastern portion of Thebes containing the sanctuaries of Amon. West Thebes' development was most extraordinary: from a necropolis, or "city of the dead," it developed

into a real city inhabited by the living. We shall later be looking at that phase of West Thebes, but for now we are concerned with the tombs that have earned this region the name "Valley of the Kings."

Valley of the Kings

The royal tombs were cut out of rock in the sides of a valley formed by the hills on the western bank of the Nile. Each tomb included several rooms, the last of which contained the sarcophagus with the mummy. The walls of every room were almost entirely covered with paintings (or painted low-reliefs) representing exclusively scenes of the pharaoh's life in the "other world." Based on the same principle we met as far back as King Djoser's complex at Sakkara, the symbolic-evocative power of such representations constituted a sort of companion for the king's death journey. In any case, once the funeral was over, the tomb was sealed and its entrance covered over so that no traces of it could be seen. This was done because what was in the tomb concerned only the king, and not the living.

Meanwhile, the rulers of the Eighteenth Dynasty initiated the custom of separating the mortuary temple from the tomb. They had their mortuary temples built on the plain that lies between the Nile and the west bank of hills. For a long time, scholars interpreted this separation as the desire of these New Kingdom sovereigns to hide their tombs because of the rich treasures placed therein. This may be. But this theory would seem to be shaken by the fact that the royal tombs in the Valley of the Kings were opened and looted within a few centuries after being hidden. Furthermore, a pyramid is no more easily violated than a "hidden" tomb.

No, there is probably a more political reason, resulting in a different attitude toward the dead. However, the search for a solution is complicated by the lack of archaeological remains of Eighteenth Dynasty temples. Any conclusions must be drawn from later temples — those of the Nineteenth and Twentieth Dynasties, that is — which seem to have been modelled on those of the Eighteenth Dynasty.

Recall that the essential function of a mortuary temple was to permit the communication between the living and the dead and consider that the tomb-and-temple complexes of the previous pharaohs had been inaccessible to the mass of people. Now, in the New Kingdom, the new pharaoh had his new role to play: he was to communicate more directly and more widely with his subjects. The tomb could hardly be approached by large numbers of ordinary Egyptians: there had to be, after all, boundaries to the privacy of the king-as-god's soul. But the temple could be removed from the tomb precinct and made more accessible; this could account for the New Kingdom temples on the plain, while the tombs were in the valley behind the hills.

That would also explain certain changes in the design of the traditional mortuary temple, both in the spatial layout and in the accessory furnishings. Everything would be aimed at increasing this direct contact with the people. Thus large statues of the kings were located in front of temple entrances, or at least in more accessible entrances. These statues were part of the cult that literally brought the king to his subjects.

Again, to avoid any misunderstanding, let it be said that the pharaohs of the New Kingdom did not conduct their policies in a modern

35. West Thebes: The Colossi of Memnon, statues of crystalline quartz, about 70 feet high, representing Amenhotep III and situated at the entrance of his mortuary temple, which no longer exists. Carved on the side of the throne is the symbolic representation of the Two Lands; in front, to the right of the king's leg, is a statue of his wife, Tiy. The statue to the right (in this photograph) became the center of a famous vocal phenomenon in the first century B.C., when an earthquake knocked off the top half, and for over two centuries people flocked there to hear its "music" (probably the result of expanding stone or air). But even during the Eighteenth Dynasty, the colossi had become objects of veneration.

democratic spirit. On the other hand, it is not fair to dismiss such devices as "tricks" played by the rulers upon their subjects. Every society and historical situation has to be examined on its own merits and not with the mental habits of another time or culture. We must, rather, always be aware of a particular society's internal pressures and conflicts and see how they interact and influence one another. Thus we must see the new situation of the mortuary temples in the context of the rulers' attempts to maintain unity by balancing off the country's competing forces. The power of the priests was linked to the throne by donations and tributes coming from the Near Eastern empire; the administrative organization was left in the hands of the middle class. Perhaps the most dramatic example of these new concerns was the magnificent temple of Queen Hatshepsut at Deir el-Bahri.

Queen Hatshepsut and Deir el-Bahri

Probably the first woman to have emerged into the spotlight of history through the sheer force of her person and her deeds was Hatshepsut. Admittedly, she had the advantage of being the daughter of one pharaoh, Tuthmosis I, and the wife of another, Tuthmosis II. The latter, incidentally, was also her step-brother: it was accepted in ancient Egypt that royalty could marry within the family to preserve the legitimacy and power. Then, when her husband died, Hatshepsut began to act as regent for her young nephew and stepson, Tuthmosis III. But she soon stopped functioning as an adjunct to her menfolk and began to act as the true pharaoh of Egypt — wearing the Double Crown, assuming the prerogatives of the king-as-god, and even having herself portrayed in male clothing and a ceremonial beard. Beyond such formalities, she proved herself capable of harnessing her subjects' energies, whether in undertaking trade expeditions or in constructing buildings. Perhaps the final proof of her eminence is the fact that her greatest monument is her own mortuary temple, in the place known today as Deir el-Bahri.

Deir el-Bahri is along the west bank of the Nile, just across from the site of ancient Thebes and beneath the hills that mask the Valley of the Kings. It is at a point where the rugged hills rise precipitously from the valley to a height of about 220 yards, forming a natural amphitheater of a particularly wild and imposing aspect. Like other great pharaohs of the New Kingdom, Hatshepsut had her actual tomb dug out of the rock of the Valley of the Kings behind the amphitheater of Deir el-Bahri. But her mortuary temple, the place where she would be memorialized for eternity by the Egyptian people, was given maximum prominence.

Originally, it is believed, the main complex at Deir el-Bahri was preceded by a "valley temple" close to the Nile; nothing of this exists. From this temple there ran a promenade flanked by sphinxes that led to the entrance of the mortuary temple complex that we see today. First there is a vast courtyard enclosed by a simple wall (of which little now remains); in the middle of this a large ramp with a balustrade rises to a terrace, itself forming a large courtyard. The base of the terrace is fronted by two porticoes that extend from either side of its access ramp. Rising from the center of this great terrace is another ramp that leads to a second terrace, and again twin porticoes extend

36. Valley of the Kings: Tomb of King Amenhotep II (Eighteenth Dynasty). Detail of relief on king's sarcophagus. The goddess Isis, bearing on her head the hieroglyphic sign for her name kneels in prayer on the sign for gold — indicating eternity — with her hands stretched over the sign of a seal-stamp, which also symbolizes eternity. According to the famous myth, Isis kept watch over Osiris's corpse to protect it from his wicked brother Seth; in the same way, she is being called on here to protect the corpse of the dead king, Amenhotep-as-Osiris.

from either side of that ramp to form the facade of the base of the second terrace. At the northern end of the north portico is a small sanctuary to the god Anubis, a chapel employed in the memorial ceremonies. At the opposite end of the southern portico is a sanctuary dedicated to the goddess Hathor, a celestial divinity. The actual royal mortuary chapel is dug out of the hill rock, while elsewhere around the terrace are other porticoes and sanctuaries. One of these is a solar-cult sanctuary; another is a double sanctuary dedicated to Hatshepsut and to her father, Tuthmosis I.

This latter sanctuary, incidentally, raises a special problem. Recall that the dead king was believed to become one with the god Osiris. How was it possible, then, that a royal mortuary temple consecrated to a dead sovereign, Hatshepsut, was able to accommodate the father-pharaoh of that sovereign, himself an Osiris? It seems that this temple reflects a break with the more rigid traditional theology. In other words, the temple reflects the emphasis of the New Kingdom on the personal and individual character of their rulers.

Mentuhotep III: Hatshepsut's Predecessor at Deir el-Bahri

There is much more to be learned about Queen Hatshepsut and her twenty-year reign from the remains at Deir el-Bahri and also — as so often in the study of ancient Egypt — something to be learned from the very lack of remains. Thus, Queen Hatshepsut's magnificent temple complex was not the first such construction at this locale. Five hundred years earlier, the Middle Kingdom pharaoh of the Eleventh Dynasty, Mentuhotep III, had erected his mortuary temple on this very site. In so doing, he had adopted a plan different from that employed in the construction of the mortuary complexes of the Old Kingdom. Mentuhotep's complex (which probably also included a valley temple that has disappeared under the cultivated earth and flood residue) was a series of ascending terraces surrounded by porticoes. The actual tomb was dug out of the rock under the temple complex, and on top of the highest terraces was a small brick pyramid on a brick base. As already noted with other ancient Egyptian monuments, the complex was probably built in stages that involved many changes in plans. It is suggested, for instance, that the pyramid was not part of the original conception but that someone decided to add it in order to commemorate the reunification of the nation by the Mentuhoteps of the Eleventh Dynasty. In any case, the pyramid was already being treated by the Eleventh Dynasty as a symbol and was no longer seen as an integral part of the actual tomb.

The similarities between the plan of Queen Hatshepsut's temple complex and that of Mentuhotep III's are too precise to be merely coincidental: the same terraces, the same porticoes — even something of the same relationship of the monument to the terrain (although we must be careful about reading into this our modern concept of organic architecture). In addition, there exists documentary evidence that testifies to Hatshepsut's desire to construct her temple in this place and no other, even though this meant demolishing an extensive series of tombs and monuments that were located on the plain below Deir el-Bahri.

37. Valley of the Kings: Close-up of the gold death mask of Tutankhamon (Eighteenth Dynasty). One of Amenhotep IV's immediate successors, Tutankhamon, during the course of his brief reign (he died at about 19), apparently helped to restore the Amon cult at Thebes after Akhenaton had established the Aten sun-disk cult at Amarna. Tutankhamon's was the only royal tomb found up to the present almost intact; it was discovered in 1922 by the archaeologist Howard Carter.

Queen Hatshepsut, in other words, in doing away with the mortuary complex of Mentuhotep III at Deir el-Bahri, demonstrated a firm intention to compete with her distant predecessor. It is impossible to explain exactly what her motives were. For one thing, we know so little about Mentuhotep's complex; for another, we do not know how Hatshepsut and her contemporaries regarded Mentuhotep III. Certainly he had helped to reunify the Two Lands after the First Intermediate Period, the time when the central authority of the pharaoh had been so weakened; certainly, too, his mortuary complex must have symbolized the supremacy of Thebes over the rest of the country. As to why Hatshepsut should have gone out of her way to wipe out the monuments of such a worthy predecessor, we can only advance a conjecture.

It requires us to take leave of Deir el-Bahri for a moment and to go to a place far down river, on the east bank of the Nile near Beni Hasan. There, at a site known best by its later Greek name of Speos Artemidos ("cave of Artemidos"), is an inscription famous among Egyptologists.

38. West Thebes: Tomb of Nakht (Eighteenth Dynasty). Detail of the scenes painted on the chapel walls, representing the banquet in honor of the deceased. Three seated ladies-in-waiting, with lotuses in their hands, are the object of the young servant girl's attention. Note the strange cones on the women's wigs; their function is still unknown.

In this inscription, Hatshepsut praised herself for having brought order back to the country after the appearance in the Delta of the Asians and, especially, for having revived worship in various temples in Lower Egypt. Scholarly interpretations vary, but it would appear that Hatshepsut was expressing an ambition to be credited with the restoration of traditional authority in that part of Egypt that had been dominated by the Hyksos. Yet Hatshepsut had ascended the throne a good sixty-five years after the Hyksos had been driven out of Egypt.

Returning to Deir el-Bahri, then, and her "take-over" of the site of Mentuhotep's memorial, it would seem that Hatshepsut was trying to establish an identity with the pharaoh who had earlier restored order and stability to Egypt. In other ways, too, whether in architectural details or in her own official portraits, Hatshepsut seemed determined to forge links with the Theban rulers of the Middle Kingdom. Or perhaps it was a more generalized conservative tendency in Hatshepsut's policies that caused her to identify with the past accomplishments of Egypt. Some scholars speculate that such policies

40. West Thebes: Detail of the wall paintings of the chapel of the tomb of Nakht; shown here are men picking and crushing the grapes to make wine.

41. West Thebes: Detail of the wall paintings of the chapel of the tomb of Nakht; shown here are men cutting and threshing the grain.

might have been prompted by conflict between her and her stepson, Tuthmosis III. Certainly once he gained power on his own, he pursued a different policy. Yet it would be misleading to see Queen Hatshepsut as looking only backwards to her predecessors. She was also linked to her successors in the Eighteenth Dynasty, as we shall see in further examination of her temple at Deir el-Bahri.

The Divine Birth

On the walls of certain rooms in Queen Hatshepsut's mortuary chapel, there are some paintings. They now exist in a rather precarious state, having been transmitted to us through a fairly clumsy restoration effected later, during the reign of Ramesses II. The scenes represent a sacred wedding between a god and, in this particular instance, a human being. They narrate how the god Amon, in love with the queen, Hatshepsut's future mother, presented himself as her husband and thus possessed her. From this union, Hatshepsut was born, destined to occupy the throne of the Two Lands. The scenes are accompanied by texts that relate the dialogue of the characters.

Some scholars see in these texts traces of popular story-telling, while others consider them dramatic pieces, the script for a kind of sacred play. We need not delve into such considerations, since only one fact interests us here: the desire to make the king (or queen, in this case) a divine being linked with Amon, the patron god of Thebes. Remember that, from the Fifth Dynasty onward, one of the king's titles was "son of Re," the sun god, as well as a Horus, son of Osiris. This overlapping and interweaving of different theologies and myths did not seem contradictory to the Egyptian mentality, as far as we know. The names were merely different manifestations of a single concept: the direct relationship between king and god. In this light, the sacred marriage scene of Hatshepsut's sanctuary is no surprise.

42. West Thebes: Detail of the wall paintings of the chapel of the tomb of Nakht; the men are winnowing the chaff from the wheat.

43. West Thebes: Tomb of Menna (Eighteenth Dynasty). This detail of wall paintings in the chapel shows a portrait of the deceased's wife.

HYMN OF VICTORY OF MERNEPTAH OVER THE LIBYANS

Thus speak the lords of Heliopolis about their son, Merneptah Hotep-hir-Maat: "Give him a lifetime like Re, that he may answer on behalf of him who is suffering because of any country. Egypt has been assigned to him to be the portion of him who represents her, for himself forever, so that he might protect his people. Behold, as one dwells in the time of the mighty one, the breath of life comes immediately. The valiant one, who causes goods to flow to the righteous man — there is no cheat who retains his plunder. He who gathers the fat of wickedness and the strength of others shall have no children." So they speak.

Merey, the wretched, ignorant enemy of Rebu, was come to attack the "Walls of the Sovereign," the son of whose lord has arisen in his place, the King of Upper and Lower Egypt: Ba-en-Re Meri-Amon; the Son of Re: Merneptah Hotep-hir-Maat. Ptah said about the enemy of Rebu: Gather together all his crimes, returned upon his own head. Give him into the hand of Merneptah Hotep-hir-Maat, that he may make him disgorge what he has swallowed, like a crocodile. Now behold, the swift carries off the swift; the Lord, conscious of his strength, will ensnare him. It is Amon who binds him with his hand, so that he may be delivered to his *ka* in Hermonthis; the King of Upper and Lower Egypt: Ba-en-Re Meri-Amon; the Son of Re: Merneptah Hotep-hir-Maat."

Great joy has arisen in Egypt;
    Jubilation has gone forth in the towns of Egypt.

[ANET, p. 378]

What is more important here, is that the Eighteenth Dynasty kings added Amon to the concept of regality. Until then, Amon had not been linked to the royal figure. Some scholars see in these scenes Hatshepsut's attempt to justify her ascension to the throne because she did not have any right to succession. But all the relationships within the Tuthmosis family are so complex, and so obscure, that we are unable to judge who did or did not have rights to the throne. It seems better to interpret the sacred wedding depicted at Deir el-Bahri as an official act, a sort of consecration of the new national god, Amon. This automatically raises the crucial question of the relationships between the royal power and that of the priesthood, particularly the priests of Amon in this period. We shall postpone our discussion of this point until we come to the temples of Amon.

Senmut, Hatshepsut's Chief Adviser

In the documentation we have of Queen Hatshepsut's reign, there are two particularly important elements. One of these is the sacred wedding motif. The second, however, is not a monument, but a man whose name is indissolubly linked with the queen's: Senmut, her chief and most trusted minister. Much has been written about the relations between these two, and even today there are some who search for spicy details, as if it were a case for sensational journalism. In fact, all the extant documentation on these two illustrious personages is strictly official; no ancient Egyptian would dream of recording his private affairs in an official document, least of all a queen. In any case, none of this gossip matters from a historical point of view.

What does matter is that Senmut, a state functionary, probably of humble origins, having passed through a series of administrative posts,

44. **West Thebes: Tomb of Menna. Details of the wall paintings in the chapel depict a hunt among the reeds. The dead king (left), accompanied by his wife and children, strikes the wild birds with a sort of boomerang while standing in his papyrus boat. On the right, a detail shows fishes in the papyrus swamp.**

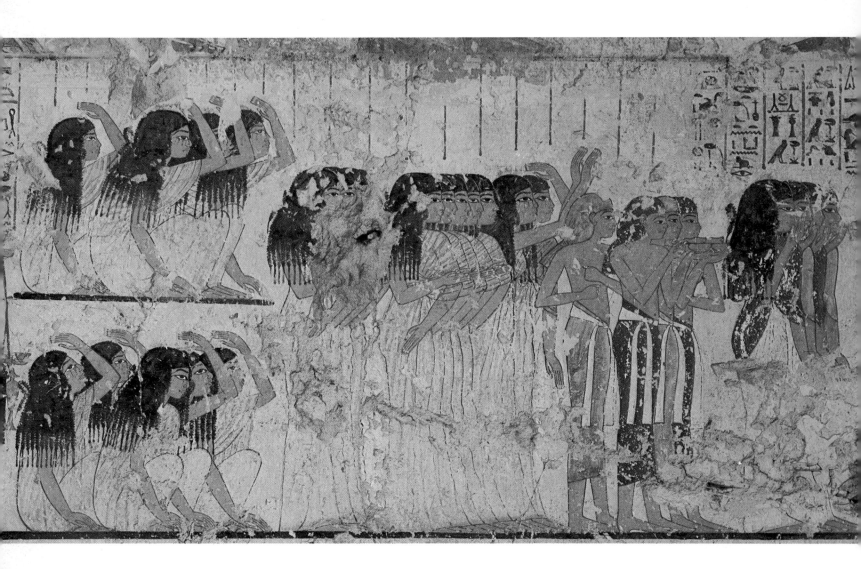

finally became the "power behind the throne." As far as we know, it was Senmut who supervised the construction of the queen's mortuary temple and probably chose the site; and the temple itself bears the stamp of his personality. This case is analogous to that of King Djoser's funerary complex at Sakkara, which is linked to Imhotep. But the situation is also different, for Senmut had no religious status, as had been the case with Imhotep, high priest of Re at Heliopolis.

Finally, it seems false to portray Senmut as the man who had to protect and sustain the fragile femininity of the queen. The idea of a woman ruling Egypt may well seem more extraordinary to us today than it did to the ancient Egyptians. Also, the role of a commoner who assists the sovereign while remaining somewhat outside the ruling hierarchy, is found again and again during the Eighteenth Dynasty, and in connection with kings who were neither "fragile" nor "feminine."

The Enduring Power of the Sun God

We have tried to focus on some of the elements crucial to an evaluation of Queen Hatshepsut's career, especially as they are revealed by the monuments of her reign. She also made some contributions to the great temple of Amon at Karnak, on the east bank of the Nile, but these are best seen later when we discuss the growth of the temple as a whole. Hatshepsut's successor, Tuthmosis III, also made some contributions to the temple at Karnak, but he is often best known as the pharaoh who methodically obliterated Hatshepsut's name from her

43. West Thebes: Tomb of Ramose (Eighteenth Dynasty). Detail of the chapel wall paintings, here depicting the funeral procession.

46. **West Thebes: Tomb of Ramose (right),** showing the interior of the chapel. In the background is the western wall with the painting of the funeral procession. On the left, the southern wall, on which are reliefs depicting the banquet in honor of the dead king.

West Thebes: Tomb of Ramose
1 *Access ramp*
2 *Courtyard*
3 *Transverse room*
4 *Longitudinal room*
5 *Subterranean burial chamber*

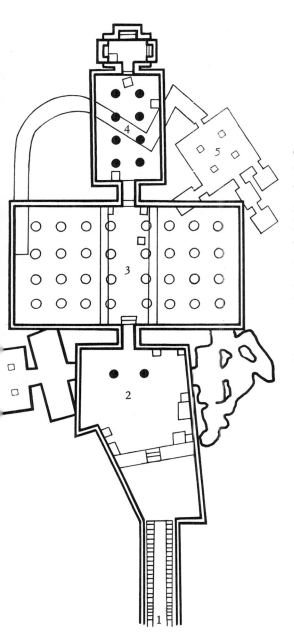

own monuments, his revenge for her twenty-year usurpation of his throne. Such "erasures" were not at all uncommon in ancient Egypt where the word and reality, the name and the person, were considered inseparable. What truly distinguished Tuthmosis III in his day were his numerous military campaigns in Palestine and Syria, through which he established an empire. We have already discussed what this empire actually meant to New Kingdom Egypt, just as we have anticipated the growth of the army, the bureaucracy, and the clergy that accompanied Tuthmosis III's reign. We shall refer to his monuments later, but we should point out here that he had much to do with turning Egypt outward and allowing his people to interact more with foreign cultures.

It was during the reign of Tuthmosis III's great grandson, Amenhotep III, that the Eighteenth Dynasty led Egypt to its greatest affluence, thanks to the peace and commerce that extended throughout most of the new empire. Amenhotep III also revived the practice of building ambitious monuments, including many temples, and we shall soon be viewing some of these. But it was under his son, Amenhotep IV, that Egypt passed through one of its most unusual phases. He decided to revive the old image of the pharaoh-as-god and to impose his primacy over the increasingly influential clergy. As so often in Egyptian history, a change in pharaonic policy was accompanied by a shift of the capital: Amenhotep IV moved his court to Amarna, about two hundred miles north of Thebes, a site now known as Tell el-Amarna. There he replaced the worship of the god Amon with the cult of Aten, a god represented by the sun disk and promoted as a single and universal deity accessible only through the pharaoh-as-god. Amenhotep IV even changed his name to Akhenaten, removed the name and image of Amon from monuments, and confiscated the goods of the other gods' temples.

But as fascinating as Akhenaten would be in another context, his reign — known as "the Amarna period" — has less importance for our purposes because of its scarcity of monuments. When he died, Thebes once more became the capital, and his court at Amarna was allowed to fall to ruins. What concerns us is to place Akhenaten and his cult of the sun-disk into the broader patterns of Egyptian history. The fact is, sovereigns of the Eighteenth Dynasty had shown interest in Re, god of the sun, long before Akhenaten concentrated on the sun-disk. What this devotion to the sun meant is difficult to say precisely, but we get a clue by once more turning to certain monuments.

The Colossi of Memnon

In front of the entrance to Amenhotep III's mortuary temple, at West Thebes, two colossal monolithic statues of the king were placed. Originally some seventy feet high, these two statues, now faceless, have been known as the Colossi of Memnon ever since the early Greeks linked them to a mythical king of Ethiopia. In their inscriptions there appears for the first time the regal appellation "prince of princes." We know that these statues had a religious significance, and we also know that later, during the Nineteenth Dynasty, King Ramesses II built similar statues which were also objects of worship and were inscribed with both the appellations "prince of princes" and "Re of princes." Moreover, as far as we know, Amenhotep III was the first Egyptian ruler who had at least one temple built — at Soleb in Nubia — where he was worshiped as a divinity. Keeping in mind other aspects of the Eighteenth Dynasty — the glorification of the pharaoh's physical strength by Tuthmosis III and Amenhotep II; Amenhotep III's delight in having himself portrayed with his wife, Queen Tiy; the introduction of the colossal in statuary; and the celebration of the military achievements of the king on temple walls — we can understand how all this led to one end: the pharaoh had become a unique and solitary figure, divine not only by virtue of representing the living renewal of the eternal myth of Horus, avenger of his father Osiris, but also divine in a freer, more immediate manner, one that was accessible to almost everyone.

It was this latter aspect — the availability of the god-king to the masses — that allowed the pharaoh to aspire to a universality tinged with strong political motives. That was how the king became the real creative force of society in the New Kingdom. It was he who guaranteed the application of the laws, who made all decisions, who "listens to the prayers" — and, naturally, answered them. We can therefore interpret the association with the sun god, Re, as a harking back to the most potent aspect of Egyptian divinity. The god-king of the Old Kingdom had been mute and inaccessible to the masses; his actions were not publicly accounted for because they were part of a rigid theological structure. The god-king of the New Kingdom, however, was a public god (in this sense, a development of an idea that germinated in the Twelfth Dynasty, as we have seen) who spoke about everything, who was interested in everything and everyone, without intermediaries. We shall see the final development of this process when we come to the Nineteenth and Twentieth Dynasties.

The Tombs of the Notables

Up to now, in our survey of the Eighteenth Dynasty, we have focused almost exclusively on the figure of the pharaoh and the way his new role was expressed in the monuments. Yet we have also had to be continually aware of the new relations and political pressures that contributed to the balance of forces during this period. We have glimpsed the middle class's place in the new scheme of things. But whereas there are many royal and official texts that explicitly confirm the image of the pharaohs projected by their monuments, what we know about the middle class must be deduced from the monuments left by its representatives. As with the pharaohs, most of these monuments were tombs, and just as the new rulers abandoned the pyramid tomb of the Old Kingdom, so the functionaries no longer constructed mastabas typical of their predecessors.

Most of the middle class notables built their tombs in West Thebes. But while the pharaohs' tombs were concentrated in the Valley of the Kings, and those of the queens in the nearby Valley of the Queens, the functionaries' tombs were spread everywhere, cut out of the sides of the hills that mark the border of the plain that stretches along the west bank of the Nile. And these functionaries' tombs are visible from the plain, not hidden as were the royal tombs.

There was a reason for this. Remember that the essential part of the worship of the dead was the presentation of the offerings. We have already seen how, at that point during the Fifth Dynasty coinciding with the growth of the high functionaries' power, the structures used for such a rite assumed predominant importance in the mortuary complex. The conception of the soul's survival, and the ritual of offerings, was maintained throughout the following centuries. What should also be noted is that the plan of the rock tombs (or hypogeums) of the Eighteenth Dynasty functionaries can roughly be derived from that of the Old Kingdom mastabas, although the latter was built up with stone blocks rather than cut out of the rocky hills. However, the development of this plan does not interest us so much as the fact that the new structures served specific functions. The typical Theban hypogeums of this period consisted of two parts: the actual burial chamber in which the sarcophagus and funerary furnishings were placed, and the chapel. The first was situated at the bottom of a shaft that, like the chamber, was cut out of the natural rock. The shaft at the top opened onto one of two upper rooms, also entirely cut out of the rock. These two rooms, in general long and narrow, were cut in a "T" shape. The fundamental difference between the royal tombs and those of private citizens were those two rooms; they were actually the part that corresponded to the mastaba chapel. In effect, the royal tomb, being separated from the mortuary temple, had no need of a special place for the offerings. And while the lower chambers of the

47. West Thebes: Detail of a scene painted on the chapel wall in the tomb of Ramose. Depicted here is the funeral procession in which a group of women manifest their grief.

notables' tombs were closed once the funeral was over, and the shaft opening carefully walled up and hidden in the chapel floor, the chapel remained accessible to the deceased's relations for the presentation of the offerings.

The Wall Paintings in the Notables' Tombs

Of primary importance in these tombs is the fact that the walls of the two chapel rooms were generally decorated with paintings and reliefs. The great number of tombs preserved, the continuity of time they represent, the uniformity of style they reveal — all these factors make them precious monuments from an archaeological, religious, and historical point of view, as well as works of art. Attempts have been made to establish a standard criterion in the choice of the subjects or the positions of these representations. But despite these paintings' apparent similarities and the uniformity that every Egyptian artist brought to his work in an entire series of fixed subjects and models, there are practically no two Theban tombs that have the same scenes, organized in the same way and in the same place. If to the untutored eye all these scenes seem the same, an Egyptologist will never confuse one tomb with another.

It is precisely for these reasons that the Theban notables' tombs represent such an exceptional document. Evidently we are looking at a series of works by painters who were never content with what tradition furnished them with, but who constantly sought new solutions. This is not surprising, as the artisans of the Eighteenth Dynasty were among the best in Egypt's history and were probably the same ones who worked with the royal painters and sculptors, or were at least from the same school. In this sense, we can speak of a Theban style of painting. What can we learn from these Theban tomb decorations? From the point of view of content, we can divide the subjects into two basic groups: one that deals with the deceased's activity during his life, the other that describes his funeral. The first group decorates the walls of the first chapel room (the transverse part of the "T") and the second decorates the longitudinal chamber. It is clear that the first group – – the deceased's activities while alive — offers the greater possibility for new ideas and variations. And this is one of the reasons they have become world famous, so much so that they condition our image of ancient Egypt. (For example, in Verdi's *Aida*, the ballet scene has traditionally been based on postures and costumes found in the Theban tomb paintings.) We are thus in possession of a collection of material depicting almost all the everyday activities of the period.

Now, we have already noted in the mastabas what such representations meant. But if the person who commissioned these later paintings had in mind something that was to promote his life in the next world, we must consider them in a different way. When a state functionary represented what was to be his future life on the walls of his tomb, he wanted these figures to illustrate not so much the reality of his daily life as that which, in his opinion, should have been the reality. We stress this point because one often reads that these scenes reveal a

Regulation laid upon the vizier, Rekhmire. The officials were brought to the audience-hall. His majesty commanded that the vizier, Rekhmire, be presented for appointment for the first time.

His majesty spake before him: "Take heed to thyself for the hall of the vizier; be watchful over all that is done therein. Behold, it is a support of the whole land; behold, as for the vizier, behold, he is not sweet, behold, bitter is he, when he addresses. Behold, he is not one setting his-face toward the officials and councilors, neither one making brethren of all the people. Behold, a man is in the dwelling of his lord, he does good for him.

Behold, the petitioner of the South, the North and the whole land, shall come, supplied. Mayest thou see to it for thyself, to do everything after that which is in accordance with law; to do everything according to the right thereof. Behold, as for an official, when he has reported water and wind of all his doings, behold, his deeds shall not be unknown. He is not brought in because of the speech of the responsible officer, but it is known by the speech of his messenger as the one stating it; he is by the side of the responsible officer as the speaker; he is not one lifting up the voice, a messenger petitioning or an official. Then one shall not be ignorant of his deeds; lo, it is the safety of an official to do things according to the regulation, by doing that which is spoken by the petitioner.

It is an abomination of the god to show partiality. This is the teaching: thou shalt do the like, shalt regard him who is known to thee like him who is unknown to thee, and him who is near like him who is far. An official who does like this, then shall he flourish greatly in the place. Do not avoid a petitioner, nor nod thy head when he speaks. As for him who draws near, who will approach to thee, do not ignore the things which he saith in speaking. Thou shalt punish him when thou hast let him hear that on account of which thou punishest him. Lo, they will say, the petitioner loves him who nods the head.

[ARE, III, pp. 268–9]

"great sense of the natural" or an "intense spirit of observation." The fact is that nowadays many people still tend to judge a painter on how faithfully he can reproduce what he sees in its most minute detail.

But, in fact, the Theban paintings have nothing at all to do with realism as we know it today. On the contrary, they are rigorously schematic illustrations. Essentially, they narrate a series of technical procedures by which certain things were accomplished. Therefore, it seems dangerous to extract from such pictures any data that are not strictly related to these rituals, or at least to the ambitions of the person who commissioned them. And as for reconstructing the mentality of the ancient Egyptian farmer, his way of life, his needs and aspirations — here, too, these tomb paintings must be viewed in the context of the society that produced them. For example, if we see a painting of a farmer happily cutting grain, we can not necessarily deduce that Egyptian farmers lived in a land of plenty. The owner of the tomb was the functionary responsible for the collection of taxes. There being no money at the time, these taxes took the form of a certain quantity of grain. It was most certainly in the interest of the deceased to show how under his control the fields produced exceptional crops, and how calm and disciplined tax collections were, almost as if the farmers under his administration spontaneously offered to "pay up," so happy were they to work for such a good and just administrator.

The Gods in Egyptian Religion

This brief view of the tombs of the Theban notables and the function of their interior decorations brings us face to face with the essence of Egyptian religious life: concern for the eternal life, whether of the functionaries, royalty, gods, or some less tangible spirit This, in turn, will lead us to examine the temples in which this concern was expressed through ceremonies and rites. But before exploring the physical details of the temples, we should know something more about the religious beliefs of the ancient Egyptians. Considering the prominence given to various deities and religious motifs in Egyptian art and documents, there are surprisingly large gaps in our knowledge of these ancient religious beliefs. Theological texts are rare; the Pyramid Texts of the Old Kingdom, for instance, must be used with extreme care because they were subordinated to the specific end of guaranteeing the future life of the king. What we know of religion in pharaonic Egypt consists mostly of the rituals and the organization of the clergy.

Still, we have established that every pharaoh was assumed to possess a *ka* and that this *ka* corresponds in certain respects to our idea of the "soul." Here, too, it is difficult to provide precise details. It seems certain, though, that the entire ritual of the offerings at a mortuary temple was conceived in connection with the *ka*; the ritual's aim was to assure the survival of the king. The *ka*, in order to live, needed daily offerings.

We have compared the *ka* to the soul, but the first thing that differentiates the concept of the *ka* from our religious concepts is that the former was tied to the earth first and foremost. Even a *ka* of an Egyptian god had had to be maintained through offerings. One consequence of this was that, for the ancient Egyptian — at least in their religious beliefs — the separation between soul and body did not take place with anguish. Rather it was only a superficial separation; with the offerings, the Egyptian was assured of the means of sustaining his eternal life.

Within limits, the same was true of a god. The god's *ka* could appear on the earth at will, providing he found a settling place for it — that is, a home. Just as the *ka* of a dead person could "live in" the tomb, so the god's *ka* had the temple. And again, just as in the tomb the paintings served as a reference point for the *ka*, so in the temple the paintings of the god served the same purpose. In the same way that the ancient Egyptians planned for the eternity of the individual, they expressed their relations with the gods. It is for this reason that the Egyptians never appear to be at the mercy of the gods; conversely, these relations never assumed the dramatic character of other religions.

Another aspect of Egyptian religion is the role of the sacred animals. Almost every god could be represented by a certain animal (for example, Amon by the ram, Thoth by the ibis, Horus by the falcon, and so on) without that animal being considered exactly an incarnation of the god. We do not know the origin of this characteristic of Egyptian religion; it must certainly have very ancient roots, probably preceding the unification of the country. We might speculate on an age when politically independent groups of people expressed their religious beliefs through animal cults, or a certain type of totemism. What matters is that from the outset of the historical period there had been established that relationship to sacred animals that was to remain characteristic of ancient Egypt. Very likely we attach more importance to the presence of such animals than the ancient Egyptians themselves did.

The Absence of Sacrifices

Perhaps the most important characteristic of ancient Egyptian religion was the absence of sacrifices, which signifies the absence of a sense of guilt, the absence of any form of purification or moral redemption. Contrary to what is generally believed, the Egyptians were basically·untouched by any religious "problem." This should not be surprising if we remember that their religious experience was the expression of a society organized under a centralized national state, with extremely clear and simple relationships, so simple that the Egyptians were able to carry them on for millenniums, adapting them from time to time to changing needs. And just as the duty of the good functionary was to carry out his job most scrupulously, so the typical moral ideal of ancient Egypt was just that calm, day-by-day performance of one's job as best one could. The Egyptians gave the name *Maat* to this sense of order and balance, personified by a beautiful goddess who stood for what we would call justice, truth, rightness. Therefore we might well replace that idea of an Egypt in which the secular functions are carried out in the name of the gods, with the opposite idea: a nation in which the religious functions were carried out according to principles much more secular than religious.

48. Abydos: Temple of Seti I (Nineteenth Dynasty). We are looking at the second courtyard, as seen from the north. To the right rear, the entrance to the sanctuary, preceded by an arcade. Of the seven original doors, only two are now open; Ramessess II (Nineteenth Dynasty) closed the others by a wall covered with inscriptions.

Abydos: Temple of Seti I
1 Entrance
2 Courtyard
3 Courtyard
4 Hypostyle hall
5 Sanctuary

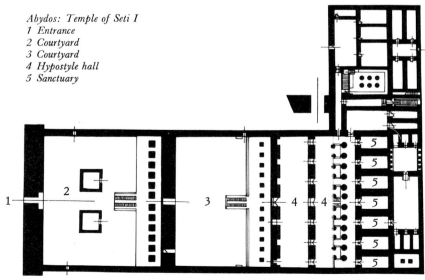

The Temple as the House of God

The religious life of the ancient Egyptians, at least as far as we can recreate it today, was focused on the temples. The texts that deal with the temple embellish its origin with a series of mythological elements. Thus, a temple was directly connected to the moment of the world's creation: from the primordial waters of Chaos there emerged a little hill, the first earth, on which the god-creator found refuge (this god varying according to the temple that elaborated the creation myth). For the historian, it is difficult to distinguish the symbolical elements from those that were originally functional and only later wrapped in mythical garb. However, the Egyptian word for temple clearly indicates that it is a house of the gods. We cannot say with certainty to what extent the temple plan corresponded with the plan of a typical Egyptian house. But without taking the term too literally, we may say that the temple was for a god what a house is for man.

If the temple was seen as a house, then the major ritual performed in the temple — namely, the presentation of offerings — must fit into that concept. Now, in many ancient religions, sacrifice was the major ritual. The concept of sacrifice implies a direct relationship between

the sacrificer and the sacrificed, which can lead to direct contact with the god himself. The victim "takes the place" of the sacrificer, otherwise the sacrifice would not make sense. The fact that in the Egyptian religion the function of sacrifice is replaced by offerings is most important. It suggests that there existed an almost qualitative distance between divinity and the human condition, a gap in which the offerings were little more than a passive link rather than an active and vital agent in the relationship. Now, the Egyptians viewed their gods as the owners of the universe, the earth in particular. Offerings can thus be seen as a presentation of "rent" by the farmers (human beings) to the landlords (the gods). In this sense, the secular patterns of religious worship become highly significant. Evidently the official cult was the formal expression of the Egyptian ruling class, and hence of those who had a monopoly of the means of production — in this case, the land owners.

We may recall an example to prove this point: the myth of Osiris. The spread of the cult of this divinity on a national scale took place between the Old and Middle Kingdoms, just when the central power was practically non-existent. The Osiris myth included a passion

51. Abydos: Detail of the wall paintings in the temple of Seti I, in which King Seti I, wearing the "blue crown," prays before an altar and receives from the gods life, stability, power, and the "renewal of millions of years," symbolized by their respective hieroglyphic signs.

motif, the sacrifice of the god himself, following a pattern found in various religions: the tendency of man to "make himself a god," to relive the passion, and to eliminate that qualitative distance we spoke of before. We can therefore easily understand how Osiris, during this period in particular, became the popular god *par excellence*, the god every man aspired to become. This attempt to deify the individual can then be interpreted as the rejection by the non-owner social classes, of the reality in which they lived and their desire for a better fate, if not in this world, at least in the next. Conversely, the popularity of the Osiris myth and cult confirms that the temple was strictly an "official" precinct — that is, one belonging to the ruling class. Popular cults did not express themselves in forms — or at least not until the Nineteenth Dynasty — that have left concrete archaeological remains.

Ceremonies in the House of God

The concept of the temple as the "house of god" has been accepted, with the proviso that it should not be taken too literally. But in examining the relationship between the physical elements of the temples and the ceremonies that took place therein, the concept helps to illuminate Egyptian religious attitudes. Some such relationship is inherent in all religious structures, of course, even when the concepts and the temples differ greatly from those of the ancient Egyptians, as in Christianity. In the classical Greek temple, for example, the statue of the god was retained but the altar was situated in an area in front of the temple; the same happened with the ancient Roman temple. And in these two civilizations, not only did the most important moment of worship, the sacrifice, take place outside the temple, but it occurred on certain occasions only.

In Egypt we find the opposite situation. If we consider the presentation of the offerings as analogous to the sacrifice, it took place inside the temple, and it was a part of a series of ceremonies carried out every day inside the temple. Only on certain days of the year, when there were holidays or anniversaries, did the god — that is, his statue — leave the temple to visit other sanctuaries in a grand procession. In this kind of calculated, organized worship, there is no room for any really autonomous action on the part of the god — that is, his priests. Once again we note the paradoxically secular, almost governmental aspect, represented here by the organization of the clergy. This, as we have said before, is in complete contrast with the traditional vision of ancient Egypt, according to which everything was dominated by superstition.

The daily ritual inside a temple provides a clearer picture of this secular routine. Every day there occurred what occurred in a private home. The owner — that is, the god — incarnate in the sanctuary statue, was awakened at dawn. There then followed the presentation of the offerings, a kind of "breakfast." When the god was satisfied, the secondary gods and other particularly important personages who enjoyed the privilege of having a statue in the temple took what remained. The priest then proceeded to prepare the god's "toilet" — that is to say, the clothes from the day before were taken off and washed and new ones were put on the statue. Then at noon there was the sprinkling and burning of incense. At sunset more offerings were presented.

PROVERBS AND PRECEPTS FROM
INSTRUCTION OF AMEN-EM-OPET

TWENTIETH CHAPTER:
Do not confuse a man in the law court,
Nor divert the righteous man.
Give not thy attention only to him clothed in
　white,
Nor give consideration to him that is unkempt.
Do not accept the bribe of a powerful man,
Nor oppress for him the disabled.
As for justice, the great reward of god,
He gives it to whom he will. . . .
Do not falsify the income on the records,
Nor damage the plans of god.
Do not discover for thy own self the will of
　god,
Without reference to Fate and Fortune. . . .
TWENTY-FIFTH CHAPTER:
Do not laugh at a blind man nor tease a dwarf
Nor injure the affairs of the lame.
Do not tease a man who is in the hand of the
　god,
Nor be fierce of face against him if he errs.
For man is clay and straw,
And the god is his builder.
He is tearing down and building up every
　day
He makes a thousand poor men as he wishes
Or he makes a thousand men as overseers,
When he is in his hour of life.
How joyful is he who reaches the West,
When he is safe in the hand of the god.
[ANET, p. 424]

52. Abydos: Detail of the reliefs on the walls of the temple of Seti I. Prince Ramesses (later King Ramesses II) adds two rolls of papyrus to the list of kings who lived before his father, Seti I; part of this list can be seen to the right of the figure.

53. Abydos: Temple of Ramesses II. Detail of the wall reliefs of the temple, representing phases of the worship ceremony. The personifications of the various districts of the nation bear tables with offerings; hanging from their arms are hieroglyphic signs, the *ankh*, signifying life.

54. Abydos: Temple of Ramesses II (Nineteenth Dynasty) is seen from the southeast.

That is, generally speaking, the essence of the administration of a temple. Not everybody could have access to the god, who was enclosed in a kind of stone tabernacle, its sealed doors were opened every morning and sealed again after the ceremony. In general only one priest carried out the functions that implied direct contact with the god. Yet it is obvious that this type of ritual presupposes an entire series of physical structures (such as storerooms for the keeping of the food to be used in the offerings, the god's clothes, trays and vases for the offerings, and so on) and administrative structures (for there must have been one particular type of priest for every duty connected with the worship practice). Thus the more important the god and the temple, the more numerous the staff. And, indeed, it is known that the staff of the temple of Amon at Karnak during the Nineteenth Dynasty consisted of a seemingly infinite number of persons, all called "priests," each of whom had a specific job to do. And once we have established that the ancient Egyptian priests had certain technical or practical jobs to perform, it follows that the priest as such was not a person invested with any special truth, nor was it his duty to conduct a morally exemplary life. Basically, the priest was an administrator; he was one of the god's "servants" (as an ancient Egyptian expression terms him). The clergy therefore represented neither more nor less than one of the bureaucratic apparatus of the state.

55. Karnak: The sanctuary of Amon, seen from above the first pylon and looking through the first courtyard. In the center is Amenhotep III's colonnade (Eighteenth Dynasty), at the sides of which Ramesses II (Nineteenth Dynasty) had the great Hypostyle Hall constructed. Further along, in the center, is the obelisk of Tuthmosis I.

HYMN TO AMON COMPOSED BY THE PAINTER MERISEKHMET

Praise to thee, Amon-Re-Atum-Harakhti, who spoke with his mouth and there came into being men, gods, cattle, and all goats in their totality, yea and all that flieth and alighteth.

Thou didst create the regions and the Hanebu, they being settled in their towns; also the fertile meads made pregnant by the Nun and later giving birth; yea, also good things without limit of their number to be sustenance for the living.

Valiant art thou as a herdsman tending them for ever and ever. Thus are bodies filled with thy beauty, and eyes behold through thee, and thy fear is upon everyone. Their hearts are turned unto thee. Good art thou at all times. All mankind live by the sight of thee.

Everyone saith, we are thine, valiant and timorous in one company, the rich like the poor with one voice; and everything speaketh likewise. Thy sweetness is in all their hearts. No body lacketh of thy beauty.

Do not the widows say, "Our husband art thou", and the babes "Our father and mother" The rich boast concerning thy beauty, and the poor adore thy face. The prisoner turneth towards thee, and he that hath a malady calleth unto thee.

Thy name will be protection for every lonely one; safety and health for him that sails upon the waters, rescuing from the crocodile; a memory good at the moment of turmoil, rescuing from the mouth of fever. Everyone hath resort to they presence that they may make supplication to thee.

Thine ears are open to hear it and to do their will. Our Ptah who loves his craft. Herdsman that loves his herds. Verily his prize is a good burial to the heart content with truth.

[HPBM, 3:I, p. 32]

56. Karnak: Sanctuary of Amon. The great Hypostyle Hall of Ramesses II is here seen (left) from the north-south nave.

57. Karnak: A close-up (right) of the capitals of the central columns in Ramesses II's Hypostyle Hall at the sanctuary of Amon.

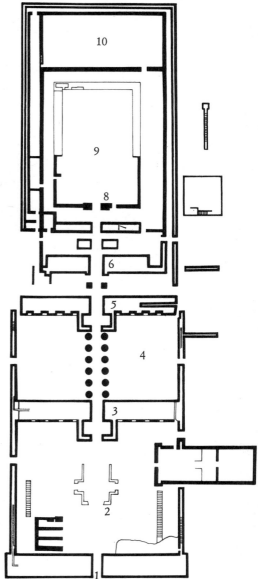

Karnak: Sanctuary of Amon
(east-west section)
  1 Entrance and first pylon
  2 Courtyard
  3 Second pylon
  4 Great Hypostyle Hall
  5 Third pylon
  6 Fourth pylon
  7 Fifth pylon
  8 Sixth pylon
  9 Sanctuary
  10 Festival Hall of Tuthmosis III

58. Karnak: Sanctuary of Amon. Detail of the reliefs on the walls of the sanctuary. In this one, King Seti I is praying, protected by the goddess Sekhmet (with a lion's head); he receives from the god Horus (with a falcon's head) life, power, and the "renewal of millions of years," as symbolized by their respective hieroglyphic signs. Note the double profile of the king, probably due to a correction by an ancient sculptor.

Relations Between State and Clergy

We have been aware that the temples and religious monuments of ancient Egypt were all the exclusive works of the pharaohs. There is a precise reason for this. Actually, there was only one true priest, one depositary of the divine will, one guarantor of the well-being of the god's land, the nation: this was the pharaoh. Thus it was that all those connected with worship practices were really subalterns. Even the high priest, the only person who could enter the god's sanctuary, was merely the pharaoh's substitute. And just as the state functionary class grew up because the king alone found it impossible to govern a nation with such complex administrative structures, so the priesthood devel-

59. Luxor: Temple of Amon, as seen from the northeast. From right to left: obelisk, colossal statues, and the pylon of Ramesses II (Nineteenth Dynasty); courtyard of Ramesses II with the Moslem mosque; pylon, colonnade, and courtyard, followed by the sanctuary — all of Amenhotep III (Eighteenth Dynasty). Note in the center, located between the huge colonnade and the Nile, the columns of the *castrum* (fortress) that the Romans installed in the temple. In the Nile (background), is one of the islands that face Thebes; beyond are the hills of West Thebes.

On the following pages:
60. Luxor: Temple of Amon. The pylon of Ramesses II, preceded by colossal statues of Ramesses II and the eastern obelisk; only the base of the western one remains, the obelisk itself having been removed in the nineteenth century to the Place de la Concorde in Paris.

oped because the pharaoh could not attend to the ceremonies of all the nation's temples.

This explains why the king was present in pictorial representations of worship as well as in those concerning the control of products or the foundation of a building. If we now consider how, for the ancient Egyptians, every pictorial or sculptural representation had an evocative power that "brought to life" what it represented (as we established at the outset), we will understand why every room, every part of the temple bears a relief decoration succinctly representing the uses of the room or structure itself. Moreover, every relief was accompanied by texts much like sub-titles. (This has allowed experts to understand what

many temple chambers were used for.) So it was that the temple became a sort of summary of the activities carried out by each pharaoh. And so, too, we can appreciate the fundamental importance these temples play in any reconstruction of Egypt's history.

Before proceeding to examine the actual layout of Egyptian temples, we should consider the issue of church and a particular state. One often reads in history books about the conflict between royal power and church power. When we modern Westerners speak of a dispute between state and clergy, it is difficult not to refer to our own historical experience in which there were real conflicts between state and church. In the case of ancient Egypt, the situation was completely different, and to understand the difference we must make a special effort to rid ourselves of our prejudices.

Let us take an example: certain scholars have interpreted the entire policy of the Eighteenth Dynasty rulers in the light of such a conflict, so that every pharaoh has been viewed as struggling against the Amon priests' ambitions to dominate the nation. However, we have tried to see the relationship in more proportion. Essentially, we have been working out what might be called a new methodology which considers the basic problems confronting Egyptian society. It is quite true that the priests of Amon at Thebes wielded imposing power. But it would be strange to think that rulers of the stature of a Tuthmosis III, just when they were enlarging the Amon temple at Karnak, would feel that they had to take steps to counteract the clergy there. Perhaps such a conflict could be found in later Egyptian history, when the central authority was so weak that the Amon priests literally administered the government. But even then the conflict does not seem to present the dramatic overtones implied by our "church versus state."

61. **Luxor: Temple of Amon.** We are here looking down the avenue of sphinxes that connects the Luxor temple to the temple of Karnak. The sphinxes are attributed to King Nectanebo I (Thirtieth Dynasty). In the background is the pylon of Ramesses II.

62. Luxor: The avenue of the sphinxes connecting the temples of Luxor and Karnak, here seen from the southeast. Across the horizon are the hills of West Thebes.

As was the case with the great mortuary complexes at the end of the Old Kingdom, the power of the priests in the New Kingdom was based primarily on the land. The state — that is, the pharaoh — gave areas of cultivable land to the temple, from which the temples could take what was necessary for the cult rituals (food, cloth, and so on) and for the priests themselves. Every time a ruler founded a new temple or built new additions to an old temple, the staff necessary to maintain these new structures increased, and so did the royal distribution of land. When the central authority was solidly in control of considerable resources (such as the mines in Nubia, or the Near Eastern empire), obviously the temples became "bigger and better." But this did not constitute such a powerful force as to crush the state's power. Within certain limits, indeed, it could represent a force that cooperated with the central authority, working side by side with it, employing large numbers of persons.

These relationships have led us to believe that if during the Eighteenth Dynasty the clergy consolidated its strength, the royal power did the same. Even the reign of Akhenaten can be interpreted in this light. This period has always been the "last trump" of those who base their vision of the Eighteenth Dynasty exclusively upon the dynamics of the king-clergy relationship, ignoring other profound aspects. The rapid failure of Akhenaten's "revolution" after his death can be taken to mean that the nation was essentially in the hands of the Amon clergy. But it can also be interpreted (we think with greater political reality) as a result of his upsetting of the political balance of the time. The royal power was not able to take over the prerogatives of the clergy simply because it lacked the structures; on the other hand, the clergy was not something superimposed on Egyptian society, but was an indispensable element in the power relations of the time. It should not

be forgotten that the king was the one true priest and that the clergy was an integral part of the state system. Hence the consistent policy of the Eighteenth Dynasty sovereigns of establishing a balance between the various parts of the nation, in the attempt to modernize the state structures and adapt them to the new needs of the society. How right the other Eighteenth Dynasty rulers were, and how wrong Akhenaten was, will be demonstrated by the Nineteenth Dynasty.

The Typical New Kingdom Temple

We have now arrived at the point where we can approach the temples of the New Kingdom as architectural constructions. One fact must be considered: every Egyptian temple was continuously subject to changes, which often meant that the old sections were absorbed by newer ones, or that certain parts were dismantled, their blocks then being used to fill up new parts or to serve as the foundations of new constructions. This last aspect of ancient Egyptian building technique has allowed us to establish the existence of still older structures in certain cases. It also means that Eighteenth Dynasty temples were changed by succeeding dynasties. But if the Nineteenth and Twentieth Dynasties altered older temples considerably, the succeeding dynasties did very little altering of the temples of those two major dynasties. It follows that the houses of worship of these two dynasties constitute the prototype for our consideration of the Egyptian temple. However,

64. Luxor: Temple of Amon. Detail of the left side of the throne of Ramesses II's colossal statue. Two representations of the god of the Nile, with their heads bearing the heraldic plants of Upper Egypt (lotus) and Lower Egypt (papyrus), link their respective plants to the hieroglyphic sign for the word "unite," thus symbolizing the unification of the Two Lands.

65. Luxor: Temple of Amon. A view of the western side of the courtyard of Ramesses II, with the colossal statues of the king set between the columns.

66. Luxor: Temple of Amon. A detail from
the temple's wall reliefs (above) depicts
butchers cutting an ox (in the upper panel)
while below them offerings are being
readied; these preparations are on behalf
of the procession for the god.

67. Luxor: Temple of Amon. Another
detail from the temple's wall reliefs (right)
shows a group of musicians in the procession
for Amon.

"prototype" in no way implies any canonical or classical criteria as regards these temples, nor any judgment whatsoever. We simply know the temple of this period better, especially from an archaeological point of view.

Before trying to make our way through the often confusing details of specific Egyptian temples, we shall first explore an imaginary prototype, or typical layout. Like the ancient Egyptians, we would do best to approach it from the Nile. Most of the temples built in the Nile Valley were near the river and directly faced it, even where the river bends. There were practical reasons for this: in ancient Egypt, most travel was by means of boats, so that by placing the temple entrance toward the river much time and effort could be saved for the constant traffic of visitors. The access road to the temple was flanked on both sides by statues, generally of sphinxes or sacred animals, between the front paws of which there were usually figures representing the king who had dedicated the construction. In the case of the animals, the significance probably lay in the protection afforded to the sovereign by the god represented by the animal. The sphinx presents a much more complex case.

The Meaning of the Sphinx

The so-called classical sphinx is a lion with a human head; the oldest example we have is the colossal one at Giza. We do not know exactly what meaning it had for the ancient Egyptians. According to some scholars, it symbolized the force and wisdom united in the person of the pharaoh; but we feel that such symbolism is alien to the Egyptian way of thinking. The Giza sphinx was at one point in history related to the sun god by the Egyptians themselves. But even this interpretation seems to have an *a posteriori* motivation and was limited to that particular case. We can safely say only that the sphinx in Egypt was always male (whereas in Greek mythology it was female), and almost always associated with the pharaoh. Moreover, a monumental sphinx was usually placed at the entrance of some edifice. Thus, as the Giza sphinx would "look after" the royal necropolis, so the sphinxes at the temple entrances looked after the access. This interpretation would seem to be supported by the fact that, in certain cases, instead the sphinxes we find lions. If we realize that both the bolts to the Egyptian doors and the mouths of the waterspouts in the temples were in the shape of a lion's head, it follows that the lion was traditionally viewed by the ancient Egyptians as the custodian of any exterior opening in a structure, especially in one of particular importance such as a temple.

There remains the question of the human head of the sphinx. The ancient Egyptian representations of gods with a human body and an animal's head are famous. It is one way, among others, of distinguishing one god from another at first sight; thus Anubis has a dog's head, Horus has a falcon's; and so on. So, too, did the classical Greeks and Romans establish physical types for their gods, and it is difficult to confuse a painting of Jupiter with one of Mercury. In the case of the Egyptian gods, the human bodies — with some exceptions — have no particular attributes; the sole distinguishing element is the animal head (although sometimes the head was human and was accompanied by a hieroglyphic sign that stated the name of the god). Beyond this, the same thing happened with all Egyptian portraits: their bodies were basically the same, while the face alone was often given individual characterization. If the same principle is valid for the sphinx, we must conclude that it represents the lion, as custodian *and* as pharaoh — that is to say, the pharaoh as custodian of the temple. This is most probable, since the king was the supreme priest and was responsible for constructing the temples, as we shall see later.

Reapproaching along the avenue of the sphinxes or sacred animals, we arrive at the area in front of the actual entrance to the temple. This had a characteristic form, the so-called pylons. The door, or gateway, with granite architrave and jambs, was flanked by two "towers" — that is, two large rectangular structures with sloping walls built on a core faced with square stone blocks (usually sandstone). These wings were then framed in concave sections with palmleaf decorations. All this formed the pylon. In front of the pylon and at the sides of the gateway were placed statues of various sizes (which generally represented the pharaoh), as well as obelisks set up in pairs. The facade of the pylon towers had vertical grooves inside which (or so we gather from representations of the period) were installed large wooden flag poles; it is not clear just what the flags signified to the ancient Egyptians.

The Interior of a New Kingdom Temple

Before entering the temple, let us again emphasize its image as a "house of god," because this is the simplest and most useful way to look at it. Consider the temple organized like a human dwelling. There is one part for private living, another for supporting services, and a third for "public reception." So with the New Kingdom temple, we have three roughly analogous parts: one where the god lives; another where the preparatory ceremonies (or functions not directly connected with the cult) take place; and the third, which is public, a place where the god and worshiper can meet. In order to avoid confusion it would be better to use the technical names for these three parts: the sanctuary, the hypostyle hall, and the courtyard.

Once past the threshold, one entered a courtyard with stone walls, often with colonnades on at least one side. This was the public part of the temple for those who had not been ceremonially "purified." Then came the hypostyle hall (its name derived from two Greek words meaning "under pillars"). This was usually a large hall with a roof supported by columns. This was the part reserved for the purification ritual which was necessary before one could enter the last and most secret part of the temple, the sanctuary. The sanctuary basically consisted of a central room for the statue of the god, and storerooms in which ritual objects were kept.

This is roughly the typical plan of the New Kingdom temple. Obviously, no two actual temples were alike, since elements could vary in form, size, and number. But before passing on to an examination of individual temples, we must make a few more general observations. To begin with, it must be noted that the temple (like any other ancient Egyptian monument) was not conceived as a unified whole; that is to

INSCRIPTION BY RAMESSES III AT TEMPLE OF MEDINET HABU

I filled its treasury with the products of the lands of Egypt: gold, silver, every costly stone by the hundred-thousand. Its granary was overflowing with barley and wheat; its lands, its herds, their multitudes were like the sand of the shore. I taxed for it the Southland as well as the Northland. Nubia and Zahi came to it, bearing their impost. It was filled with captives, which thou gavest to me among the Nine Bows, and with classes which I trained by the ten-thousand.

I fashioned thy great statue resting in its midst; "Amon-Endowed-with-Eternity" was its august name; it was adorned with real costly stone like the horizon. When it appeared, there was rejoicing to see it. I made for it table-vessels, of fine gold; others of silver and copper, without number. I multiplied the divine offerings presented before thee, of bread, wine, beer, and fat geese; numerous oxen, bullocks, calves, cows, white oryxes, and gazelles offered in his slaughter yard.

[ARE, IV, p. 114]

say, in examining any single ancient Egyptian architectural or artistic complex, we must dispense with our typically Western criteria or standards. Such value-judgments and standards prove useful when dealing with classical Greek or Renaissance monuments; with Egyptian ones, such an approach will be a hindrance and may well lead to misconceptions. Even professionals have inveighed against the lack of taste demonstrated in the construction of the Hypostyle Hall at Karnak, the Egyptians' lack of skill and experience in building techniques, or the fact that it is impossible to photograph an Egyptian monument from a proper point of view. This is quite true. In fact, it is impossible to photograph Egyptian monuments from *any* point of view, for the simple reason that there never existed a strict point of view from which one

68. West Thebes: Mortuary temple of Ramesses II (Nineteenth Dynasty). This is a view of the western part of the second courtyard; the Osiris pillars stand in front of the hypostyle hall, the columns of which can be seen behind them. Note, on the ground in the foreground, the head of a colossal statue of the king, the largest of its kind.

was expected to view them. Nothing in an Egyptian temple is there to be looked at. The Western visitor who demands harmonious symmetry and proportions should not go to Egypt (at least to view pharaonic monuments) because his requirements will never be met anywhere in that country's aesthetic heritage.

One example will suffice to prove this point. Every doorway, every column, every statue had its own name, which was different not only from every other similar element in the same temple, but also from the other elements placed in analogous positions in other temples. This was due to the fact that no element was ever determined by aesthetic needs or considerations, but originated from the exigencies of the cult itself. Consequently, every time a pharaoh had new parts added to any temple, these parts had values and functions in themselves, but never served to change the basic core of the temple, the sanctuary.. In this sense, the temple proper was the sanctuary, where the god lived and where the most important part of the worship services were conducted. It was thus the part least subject to changes or additions, and contained the most ancient structures. Even in the case of later restoration (which often occurred), the sanctuaries generally retained the fundamental lines of their original plan.

We must also acknowledge that no aesthetic or perspective function is served by the fact that the scale of the longitudinal axis of the temple is generally the same for all its parts, and that along it the passage doors

69. West Thebes: A view of the storerooms that surround the mortuary temple of Ramesses II.

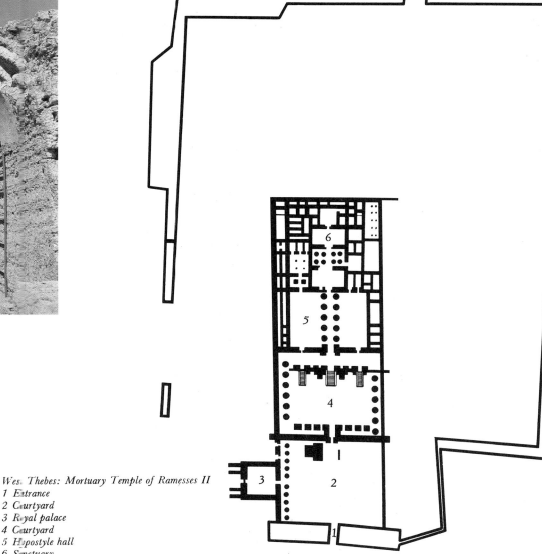

West Thebes: Mortuary Temple of Ramesses II
1 Entrance
2 Courtyard
3 Royal palace
4 Courtyard
5 Hypostyle hall
6 Sanctuary

are set in a row from one end to the other. To understand this, we need only stand at the entrance door and look toward the sanctuary: we would see a succession of doorjambs, but no rows of columns or anything else. Moreover, from what we have been able to reconstruct of the formalities of worship, there is little or nothing to indicate that ancient Egyptians entered the main door in order to go directly to the sanctuary, as we invariably do today when we visit any such monument. Most probably this alignment of doors had nothing to do with either considerations of perspective or with practical needs. Indeed, there were many instances of asymmetry. This being the case, all we can say for the moment is that the Egyptian temple of the New Kingdom includes among its characteristics a longitudinal axis on which were placed most of the doors giving access to the various other parts of the temple. And with this in mind, we can now explore one of the greatest of all the monuments of ancient Egypt, the temple of Amon at Karnak.

70. West Thebes: The head of the colossal statue of Ramesses II at his mortuary temple. Like the Colossi of Memnon and other such statues of the Eighteenth and Nineteenth Dynasties, this became an object of worship.

The Temple of Karnak

In fact, Karnak is not a temple; it is a complex of temples. Today's visitor arrives there easily from Luxor, only a couple of miles away. We have already referred to Luxor as the modern town that grew up where Thebes was; in reality the true ancient center, the heart of the New Kingdom's political and religious life, must have been Karnak. The first impression one has when crossing the threshold of the first pylon (there are many pylons at Karnak), and finding himself amid the ruins of what was the greatest ancient Egyptian sanctuary, is that he will not be able to make any sense out of it. Even the Giza pyramids, although mysterious looking, have an internal logic; they are closed up in themselves and one intuitively experiences them, even when we don't understand them. Karnak does not offer this possibility. Walking along the courtyards, rooms, columns, obelisks, statues, and miles of hieroglyphic inscriptions, the visitor soon loses any capacity to link one element or monument with another. Therefore one must return to Karnak again and again. Even then, as we have warned, he must avoid searching among the monuments with aesthetic or rational criteria — in short, modern, Western standards. And we have also said that the true temple of Amon was always the sanctuary that formed the central nucleus. All the various additions made over the course of centuries have their own value *per se*; they are separate nuclei whose presence is independently justified by ceremonial needs, by new ideological lines, or by new links between the various divinities.

We know from an inscription that at the beginning of the Middle Kingdom there was already a temple of Amon at Thebes. Nothing remains of it now, as there are few Eleventh Dynasty ruins. What we can say for certain is that the original nucleus of the temple, as we know it today, dates back to the Twelfth Dynasty, when national importance was given to the Amon cult. From what we have been able to reconstruct, the Twelfth Dynasty temple must have included three areas (oriented east-west) aligned on the principal axis and preceded by a hall (perhaps with columns) wider than it was long, which an Eighteenth Dynasty text called the "festival hall." This is all that is left of this part of Karnak.

As expected, there was a resumption of building activity at Karnak in the first part of the Eighteenth Dynasty. During the entire preceding period, the temple must have remained basically as it was during the Twelfth Dynasty. The first rulers of the Eighteenth Dynasty contented themselves with erecting small chapels, which apparently served as "stations" during the long processions of Amon's sacred boat. Tuthmosis I's additions were more important; he had a wall built round the Middle Kingdom temple; according to some scholars, this was flanked by columns that formed a sort of arcade. It is known for certain that Tuthmosis I left the sanctuary proper intact and that, with the same wall, delineated a vast rectangular space, perhaps a courtyard, in front of the sanctuary entrance. Finally, access to the new edifice was gained through a pylon (today known as the fifth pylon).

The construction ordered by Queen Hatshepsut marked a real turning-point for the temple of Karnak. If Tuthmosis I's work was basically a completion of already existing structures, Hatshepsut made some substantial changes. In the space enclosed by Tuthmosis's wall, the queen had a new sanctuary built, aligned with the older one, but independent from it and surrounded by a series of areas and rooms (probably used as storerooms). Then she had two granite obelisks constructed in front of Tuthmosis I's pylon.

Other important changes were effected by Tuthmosis III. It would be much too complicated and of no great use to describe them in detail. Essentially, that great pharaoh substituted a sanctuary made of sandstone for Hatshepsut's quartz-rock structure; he had a new pylon built (the sixth) between the sanctuary and the fifth pylon; and he transformed considerably the courtyards between the fourth and fifth pylons and then those between the fifth and the sanctuary. The courtyard between the fourth and fifth pylons was changed into a colonnaded room, where presumably the coronation of the king took place before he passed on to the purification ceremony and then into the sanctuary.

Except for a bit of retouching, that part of the temple of Amon between the fourth pylon and the Middle Kingdom sanctuary did not undergo any further transformations. From now on, any changes took place outside Tuthmosis I's wall. The transition point between these two phases of the life of the temple was marked by the additions of Tuthmosis III himself. Along the outer face of the northern part of Tuthmosis I's wall, Tuthmosis III had a series of chambers built, perhaps chapels or storerooms. They were then enclosed by a new wall, parallel to the preceding one, which went all around the sanctuary up to the southern end of the fourth pylon. The wall is quite a distance from the part of Tuthmosis I's wall that enclosed the sanctuary on the east; in the space created behind the sanctuary, Tuthmosis III had his so-called "festival hall."

Later Additions to
The Temple of Karnak

This is a singular monument, perhaps unique among all those preserved in Egypt. Its general orientation is not east-west like the Amon sanctuary, but north-south. It is in rectangular form, divided into two parts that go along the entire length of the structure. The western part includes a colonnaded room whose minor axis is aligned with the axis of the sanctuary of Amon; north of this room there are three

And his majesty said: "What is it then, my father Amon? Hath a father indeed forgotten his son? Have I done ought without thee? Have I not gone or stood still because of thine utterance? And I never swerved from the counsels of thy mouth. How great is the great lord of Thebes, too great to suffer the foreign peoples to come nigh him! What are these Asiatics to thee, Amon? Wretches that know not God! Have I not fashioned for thee very many monuments, and filled thy temple with my captives? I have built for thee my temple of millions of years, and have given thee my goods for a possession. I present unto thee all countries together, in order to furnish thine offering with victuals. I cause to be offered unto thee tens of thousands of oxen, together with all sweet-smelling plants.

"No good thing leave I undone in thy sanctuary. I build for thee great pylons, and I myself set up their flagstaffs. I bring thee obelisks from Elephantine, and I it is who conveyeth stone. I cause galleys to voyage for thee upon the sea, in order to fetch for thee the tribute of the countries. Mischief shall befall him who thwarteth thy counsels, but well fareth he that understandeth thee. One should work for thee with loving heart.

"I call to thee, my father Amon. I am in the midst of foes whom I know not. All lands have joined themselves together against me, and I am all alone and none other is with me. My soldiers have forsaken me, and not one among my chariotry hath looked round for me. If I cry to them, not one of them hearkeneth. But I call, and I find that Amon is worth more to me than millions of foot-soldiers, and hundreds of thousands of chariots, than ten thousand men in brethren and children, who with one mind hold together. The work of many men is nothing; Amon is worth more than they. I have come hither by reason of the counsels of thy mouth, O Amon, and from thy counsels have I not swerved."

[AESW, pp. 263–4]

chapels. The eastern section is subdivided into three parts: the southern part includes a colonnaded room surrounded by smaller rooms; the central part consists basically of three rooms aligned on their axis but oriented east-west; finally, the northern part includes a series of rooms that culminated to the north in a solar sanctuary (the same kind as we have seen in Hatshepsut's funerary temple at Deir el-Bahri).

There is one more addition of Tuthmosis III's to the Karnak complex — a sanctuary set on the general axis of the temple but behind it, on the eastern side of his boundary wall and oriented to the east. The characteristic element of this new sanctuary was that the cult centered round an obelisk. We have already seen that the obelisk was a monument closely connected to the cult of the god Re (in the Fifth Dynasty sun temples); now we note that, at least during the New Kingdom, they are set up in pairs in front of the temple entrance. The exceptional nature of the obelisk of Tuthmosis III is that it stood alone and was found inside the sanctuary. (Today the obelisk is no longer at Karnak; in A.D. 375 the Emperor Constantine II had it sent to Rome and set up in the Circus Maximus; it was later restored by Pope Sixtus V, who placed it in 1588 in the Square of St. John Lateran where it is to this day.) Another exceptional aspect of this obelisk is that in its sanctuary it was associated with a particular form of the god Amon, Amon "who listens to our prayers."

Amenhotep II and Tuthmosis IV, the immediate successors of Tuthmosis III, have left us constructions of only secondary importance. But the next pharaoh, Amenhotep III, further developed the temple, building another pylon even larger than its predecessors (now the third). This pylon is of particular importance to modern archaeologists. During the restoration work executed about fifty years ago, it was discovered that the pylon's filling was made of construction blocks belonging to older constructions that had been taken apart. Thus it was that two altars — one of King Sesostris I of the Twelfth Dynasty and the other of King Amenhotep I of the Eighteenth Dynasty — were discovered, together with fragments of Hatshepsut's quartz-rock sanctuary (replaced, as we have seen, by another by Tuthmosis III). In front of this pylon, Amenhotep III had a double row of seven columns built; they are about twenty-two yards high and provide a sort of gigantic entry to what was then the temple entrance. To conclude this account of the works effected by the Eighteenth Dynasty kings, the last of them, Horemheb, began construction of a new pylon (now the second), parallel to the third and situated where the two last columns of Amenhotep III's colonnade stand.

With this admittedly summary description, we have indicated the basic changes that constituted the development of the Karnak temple along its east-west axis. In order to avoid confusion, and also because they have little importance for the temple-complex plan, the innumerable sanctuaries and chapels found inside the boundary wall will not be mentioned. However we must mention one more development that renders Karnak unique among all the ancient Egyptian temples. This is the development of the temple along its north-south axis, justified by the presence to the south of another temple dedicated to the goddess Mut. There was thus formed a kind of "sacred way" flanked by sphinxes, along which small altars were erected (similar to those of Sesostris I and Amenhotep I discovered in the filling of the third Karnak pylon); these altars were used as stopping places for the sacred boat on which the statue of Amon was carried during processions.

71. Abu Simbel: Facade of the great rock temple, with the colossi representing Ramesses II. Note, next to the pharaoh's legs, the statues of his wife, Nefertari, and his children. With the construction of the high dam at Aswan, it was decided to remove the two temples at Abu Simbel to save them from the rising waters of the Nile. The temples were separated from the rock of the hill into which they had been hewn, and then cut into sections; then they were lifted, piece by piece, and reconstructed at a place near the original site but at a higher level; the reconstruction of the temple is here in progress. The temples were "re-inaugurated" in the autumn of 1968.

SCHOOL TEXT OF NEW KINGDOM PERIOD

Nay but if thou doest these things, thou art versed in the writings. Those learned scribes from the time of the successors of the gods, even those who foretold the future, it hath befallen that their names endure for all eternity, though they be gone, having completed their lives, and though all their kindred be forgotten.

They made not unto themselves pyramids of brass, with tombstones of iron. They knew not how to leave heirs that were children who should pronounce their names, but they made heirs unto themselves of the writings and the books of instruction which they made.

They appointed for themselves the papyrus-roll as a lector-priest, the writing-board as a loving-son. Books of instruction became their pyramids, and the reed-pen was their child. The stone-surface was their woman. Persons both great and small were made into their children, for the scribe, he is chief of them all.

There were made for them doors and halls, but these are fallen to pieces. Their *ka*-servants are gone, their tombstones covered with dirt, their chambers forgotten. But their names are pronounced because of these books of theirs which they made, inasmuch as they were good, and the memory of him who made them is for evermore.

Be a scribe, put it in thy heart, that thy name may fare similarly. More profitable is a book than a graven tombstone, than a chapel-wall firmly established. This serves as chapels and pyramids to the end that a man's name may be pronounced. Assuredly profitable in the necropolis is a name on the lips of mankind!

A man hath perished and his corpse is become dirt. All his kindred have crumbled to dust. But writings cause him to be remembered in the mouth of the reciter. More profitable is a book than the house of the builder, than chapels in the West. Better is it than a stablished castle and than a memorial-stone in a temple.

[HPBM, 3:I, pp. 38-9]

72. Abu Simbel: One of the statues of Ramesses II's wife, Queen Nefertari, next to the leg of the colossal statue of the king. To the left can be seen part of the symbolic representation of the unification of the Two Lands, which decorates the right side of the throne of the colossus.

73. Abu Simbel: One of the statues of the children of Ramesses II that stands at the leg of the king before the facade of the temple. Note the hairstyle, typical of children in ancient Egypt.

Later, the part of the sacred way between the central body of the temple of Amon and the boundary wall (the one surrounding the entire area in which are found the various sanctuaries that make up the complex) was set up as a series of courtyards separated by pylons. We thus have the seventh and eighth pylons (constructed under Tuthmosis I and II, Hatshepsut, and Tuthmosis III) and the ninth and tenth pylons (built by Horemheb).

The Temple of Luxor

We have stressed that Karnak is not a temple but a complex of temples; certainly there are a great many constructions of every size within the boundary wall space. Moreover, other temples adorned the city of Thebes outside the boundaries of the temple of Amon, even if they can be considered "dependent" upon the Karnak sanctuary proper. Thus, to the north, an avenue of sphinxes leads to a temple dedicated to the god Montu, just as another to the south leads to the above-mentioned temple of Mut. A second avenue of sphinxes, roughly parallel to the preceding southern one, connected the boundary of Karnak to another temple, much smaller, less complex, and not nearly

74. Abu Simbel: Facade of the minor, or smaller, rock temple, with the colossi representing Ramesses II and his wife, Queen Nefertari. Note, next to their legs, the figures of their children. This view shows the reconstruction of this temple on its new site in progress.

75. Abu Simbel: One of the colossal statues of Ramesses II on the facade of the minor rock temple.

so rich in historical remains as Karnak. Nonetheless, for the originality of its plan, for the better state of its preservation in certain places, and for the suggestiveness of its reflection in the Nile waters, this temple is one of the most popular tourist attractions. This is the temple of Luxor.

If the essential part of Karnak is indissolubly linked with the names of Hatshepsut and Tuthmosis III, Luxor bears Amenhotep III's signature. In this case, as at Karnak, we must accept the possibility of a Middle Kingdom sanctuary, here existing in the area where Amenhotep III's temple later rose; furthermore, Tuthmosis III had constructed some chapels that were later incorporated into the court-yard of Ramesses II. However, Amenhotep III deserves most of the credit for having given the sanctuary the monumental form it has today.

76. **Medinet Habu: Mortuary temple of Ramesses III (Twentieth Dynasty). A detail of the reliefs carved on the principal pylon. The king, on the left, is about to sacrifice his Asian prisoners, whom he symbolically holds by the hair, in the presence of the god Amon-Re.**

77. **Medinet Habu: Another detail of the reliefs carved on the principal pylon of the mortuary temple of Ramesses III. The king, at left, standing on a small chariot drawn by horses and accompanied by archers, hunts wild bulls along the bank of a river; note the fish in the lower right section.**

The Eighteenth Dynasty temple of Luxor has some peculiar details. If one proceeded along the avenue of sphinxes that connected it to the Karnak temple, he would reach a pylon (now mostly destroyed) in front of which were set some colossal statues of the king. The door did not lead directly into the colonnaded courtyard, but rather afforded access to a sort of long corridor surrounded on three sides (north, east, and west) by a double row of columns; the south side had four rows of columns, thus becoming a kind of colonnaded atrium. Then one entered the temple proper, which consisted of two successive hypostyle halls from which one reached the "chapel of the boat" (where the sacred boat of Amon was placed after the procession). Both the hypostyle hall and the chapel of the boat were flanked by other rooms. Behind the chapel of the boat and on the same axis, there was a third hypostyle hall, much wider than it was long; finally, again on the temple axis, there was the sanctuary proper, which enclosed a colossal statue of Amon. However the door between the hypostyle hall and the sanctuary did not exist then; it was opened only much later (probably in the Ptolemaic period), when the columns of the boat chapel were removed and replaced by a chamber with two entrances. In the Eighteenth Dynasty temple, and perhaps up to the Ptolemaic period, one could enter the sanctuary only by going around through the rooms east of the boat chapel.

Architecture and Policy in New Kingdom Temples

We have sketched these rather detailed "blueprints" of the great New Kingdom temples so that we can now proceed to set these monuments within their broader framework. The architecture of the sanctuary embodies the rulers' philosophy. From this, too, we see how important archaeology is for the historical reconstruction of the past, and how important a historical perspective is to archaeological research. Karnak's complexity shows us how many different policies and patterns of behavior can be reflected in a series of construction. Each

Medinet Habu: Mortuary Temple of Ramesses III
1 Entrance
2 Courtyard
3 Royal palace
4 Courtyard
5 Hypostyle hall
6 Sanctuary

78. **Medinet Habu: The mortuary temple of Ramesses III (below) viewed from the top of the main pylon to the east. In the foreground is the first courtyard with the Osiris pillars on the right and the facade of the royal palace on the left. This courtyard is followed by the second pylon, then another courtyard, and finally the sanctuary.**

79. **Medinet Habu: The entrance gateway (right) to the fortified boundary wall that surrounds the mortuary temple of Ramesses III; the gateway is constructed in the form of a fortress tower.**

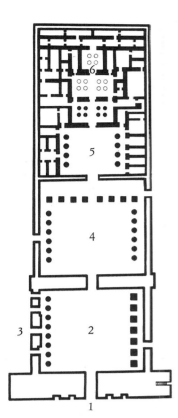

remodeling was a new expression of power and of the relationship with the gods, with the ruling class, or with the clergy. The fact that practically every sovereign, from the Middle Kingdom pharaohs to the Roman emperors, left testimony of himself at Karnak confirms the constant preoccupation with the "house" of the national god, Amon.

We must infer much because we lack documentation of many of the changes in policies. But allowing for the fragmentary nature of the evidence, we can make some interesting connections. We have seen, for instance, how Queen Hatshepsut, particularly in the decoration of her Deir el-Bahri temple, tended to put the relationship between pharaoh and Amon on a new basis. As for her contribution to the Karnak temple, it was concentrated on the sanctuary that she had reconstructed in front of the earlier Middle Kingdom one. Unfortunately we know too little of the latter to be able to establish exactly how the temples differed. We can only say that the organization given to the Karnak temple by Hatshepsut presupposed a ritual that closely linked the figure of the king with Amon.

In the various pictures and texts inscribed on the walls of certain rooms, some moments of ritual were partially represented. In Hats-

80. Medinet Habu: Detail (left) of the southern colonnade in the first courtyard of the mortuary temple; this colonnade serves as the facade of the connecting royal palace.

81. Medinet Habu: A close-up of an architrave (right) of the arcade that gives access to the hypostyle hall of the funerary temple. Note the fine state of preservation of the painting; virtually all the reliefs and inscriptions in ancient Egyptian temples were originally painted.

hepsut's time, the pharaoh, before entering the sanctuary, had to be purified in the hall between the fourth and fifth pylons, so that the real temple entrance was this fifth pylon. In the same hall, the coronation ceremony with the two crowns, representing Upper and Lower Egypt, took place. Moreover, in this same hypostyle hall they performed the so-called "jubilee," a ceremony of ancient origin in which the king had his "vital energies" renewed, thereby strengthening his capacity to govern. The following room, beyond the fifth pylon, was the place where the king "ascended" Amon's throne; there he received from the god the power that allowed him to enter the sanctuary and thus be in the presence of the divinity. Finally, after the sixth pylon came the area of the temple where the most important part of the ceremony took place, the presentation of the offerings.

A most important change at Karnak occurred with Tuthmosis III. Besides effecting some changes in the chambers built by his predecessors, he had a new section added behind the Middle Kingdom sanctuary (to the east). The entire complex was then surrounded by a wall. This last factor demonstrates one thing: the new part built by Tuthmosis III, although from a functional point of view separate from the rest of the sanctuary, nonetheless contained it in a unique and inseparable whole. This unity is emphasized by other elements; for example, despite the fact that the new temple was fundamentally oriented north-south, the three rooms that made up the sanctuary dedicated to Amon were oriented east-west and were on the same axis as the Middle Kingdom and Hatshepsut sanctuary. This means that there existed, among the new structures, a connecting link with the preceding buildings: the relationship with Amon had not changed.

Tuthmosis III's New Policies and Karnak

On the contrary, the three rooms preceded by the hall formed the same pattern as the Twelfth Dynasty temple. In this way, Tuthmosis III reaffirmed the traditional relationship with Amon. Looking at the new temple from south to north, we see that the colonnaded hall forms a pavilion in which the royal jubilee took place. The eastern part of the temple — with the rooms of Sokaris (the funerary god) and of Amon, as well as the solar rooms — symbolically represented the fate of the king, who rises to the sun from the world of the dead. Osiris the king becomes Horus, but only through the mediation of Amon.

It is not surprising that Tuthmosis III's arrangement of the Karnak sanctuary remained practically unchanged up to the end of Egyptian history. Evidently his formulation of the relationship with the god was felt to be the proper one. Changing the axis of Amon's chambers was an attempt to balance the cult of the sun god Re and the Amon cult. The fact that Tuthmosis III had particular interest in Re is demonstrated by the single obelisk he decided to erect outside the eastern door of the Karnak boundary wall: a symbol of sun worship. In addition, Tuthmosis III erected two statues, one of Amon and the other of himself (probably bearing the title of "he who listens to prayers"). Once again, Tuthmosis III set himself alongside Amon in order to reach Re. If we stop to think that most probably this section of the temple was open to the public — that is, was the place where anyone could go to pray to the king and be "heard" — we will see the connection between the sun cult and the middle classes that, as we have seen, characterized the Eighteenth Dynasty.

The same relationship between policy and architecture is found in the Luxor temple. There, the unity of arrangement, and the fact that it did not undergo radical changes throughout the centuries, demonstrates to us how well Luxor exemplified all of the various relationships of those periods in Egyptian history. If the later pharaohs did not find it necessary to change this temple, it was principally because this temple represented no ideological or political threat. Indeed, the Luxor temple had no value independent of the Karnak temple: as Hatshepsut and Tuthmosis III had built "their" temple, so Amenhotep III built "his." In fact, Luxor represented the most secret, most strictly private part of Amon's house.

We have already noted how the most important room in the Luxor temple, the one containing the god's statue, was jealously hidden behind the chapel of the boat. The question is why Amenhotep III treated Amon's inner sanctum in such a grandiose and "showy" manner? Evidently, it was to emphasize the most intimate and human

82. Valley of the Kings: Tomb of Ramesses I (Nineteenth Dynasty). This is a detail from the wall paintings and depicts the dead king's journey into the next world.

83. Valley of the Kings: Another detail from the wall paintings in the tomb of Ramesses I. The serpent god Apopus, symbol of hostile forces, is depicted as a coiled snake the king must confront on his journey into the next world.

aspect of the god, which meant extracting it from more complex and cerebral theological formulations. The figure of the god thus assumed a more direct appeal and became more immediately accessible. Naturally, this was not intended to minimize his divinity, but rather to reinforce it. This was an attempt to strengthen the doctrine of the king-as-god, establishing it on elements more consonant with the needs of the time. Amon, a humanized God, approaches the king, a deified man.

The Roots of the Nineteenth Dynasty

We must conclude our exploration of the monuments of the first of the New Kingdom's dynasties, the Eighteenth, as well as our interpretation of how the policies of that dynasty's rulers are embodied in those monuments. But before we move on to the monuments of the Nineteenth Dynasty, we must review one other phenomenon that will help to explain how the Nineteenth Dynasty evolved from its predecessors. This phenomenon was the presence of commoners who reached the top of the administrative hierarchy, and found themselves at the king's side as ministers, counselors, or in some such invaluable role. We have discussed Senmut, who held such a position with Queen Hatshepsut, and we related him to his counterpart, Imhotep, King

84. **Valley of the Kings: Tomb of Seti I (Nineteenth Dynasty). This detail of the wall paintings depicts some of the constellations.**

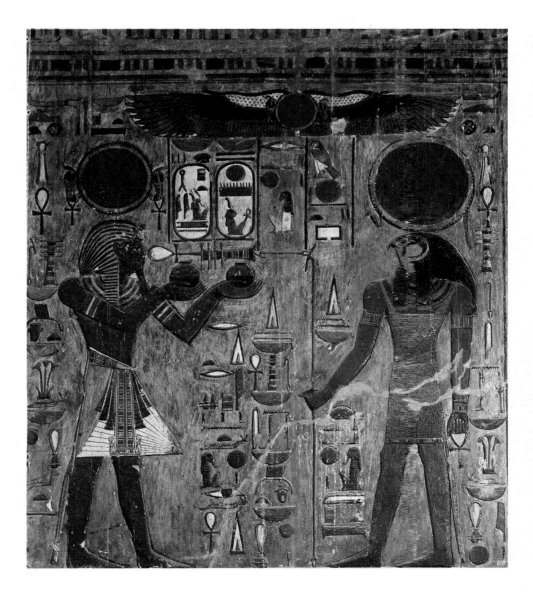

85. Valley of the Kings: Another detail of the wall paintings in the tomb of Seti I. The king, on the left, presents offerings to the god Re-Harakhte, right, with a falcon's head, who gives the king life, stability, and power, as symbolized by the hieroglyphic signs.

Djoser's chief assistant back in the Third Dynasty. There were others during the Eighteenth Dynasty, perhaps none more important than the commoner Amenhotep, Son of Hapu, who held the same position in relation to Amenhotep III.

Such figures, obviously, fit into the context of their times — specifically, with the Eighteenth Dynasty's awareness of the need for closer cooperation with the middle class and the state bureaucracy. Of more particular interest is the fact that these "new men" also held positions in the army. The role of the Egyptian army during the New Kingdom was similar to that of the clergy. Its outstanding characteristic was not so much its command of any advanced techniques or strategies, but its capacity to administrate via a highly organized bureaucracy. Thus the army officers were essentially bureaucrats, or "scribes." For example, one of the titles of Amenhotep, Son of Hapu, was "scribe of the recruits," which meant that he was responsible for conscripting the king's army.

A "scribe" in this context means not just a man who could read and write, although that skill was the first step on the new route to power. Scribe meant that the person could administrate in the fullest sense. That was certainly what Amenhotep, Son of Hapu, did, working his way higher and higher in the military bureaucracy until he became

Amenhotep III's vizier — a combination prime minister, coordinator of many sectors of public life, and adviser to the king on his personal affairs. It was Amenhotep, Son of Hapu, for instance, who supervised the estates of Amenhotep III's wife and daughter, and it was he who supervised the erection of the two statues of Amenhotep III (now known as the Colossi of Memnon) in front of the king's mortuary temple. In turn, Amenhotep, Son of Hapu, was honored by having statues of himself erected in the temple of Karnak, by having his own mortuary temple for services, and by being regarded by generations of Egyptians as a great sage.

Amenhotep III's successor, Akhenaton, seems not to have relied on any individual to this extent, for he was driven to shape his Amarna "revolution" in his own image. Then, for a few years after his death (1362 B.C.), there were three brief reigns, one by his nephew, Tutankhamon. Although Tutankhamon's life was short — he died when he was only nineteen — the discovery of his tomb-treasures seems to have brought him the eternal fame sought by all the pharaohs. The end of the Eighteenth Dynasty, however, saw another commoner reach the peak: Horemheb, at the end of the Amarna period, worked away until he took over the throne and restored the cult of Amon.

Horemheb's career before ascending the throne was centered not at Thebes, near the Amon temple and cult center, but at Amarna itself. Some scholars have been perplexed at this, since it confuses the theory of a clearly defined king-clergy conflict. On the other hand, it is proof that when a power vacuum developed, it was not filled by the Amon priests but by a representative of the middle class. This accounts for Horemheb as well as his predecessors, Senmut and Amenhotep, Son of Hapu.

Once this is established, there is no need to conjure up scenes of palace plots, internal struggles, or bloodshed in order to understand how Ramesses I, a man of humble origin who had reached the position of vizier, became pharaoh and founder of the Nineteenth Dynasty. For the mass of Egyptians, of course, the ascension to the throne of this person or that did not materially affect their lives. But the middle classes were much more concerned with such a development. As for the Amon clergy, although they represented a sizeable sector of state life, they lacked the instruments necessary to assume and maintain control — above all an army. Therefore, the rise of persons closely connected to the military sphere, and thus able to restore the "Asian policy" (a prime source of the temples' income) would also get the support of the priests as well. To these considerations we must add the fact that the middle class itself was vitally dependent on the consolidation of Egyptian power in the Near East. This explains why all the kings of the Nineteenth Dynasty — and in particular the most famous and most representative, Ramesses II — continually emphasized the warrior aspect of their persons.

It has been necessary to speak about this in order to anticipate how and why the Nineteenth Dynasty rulers' policy descended in a direct line (albeit with differences due to the changed conditions of the times) from that of the Eighteenth Dynasty. We can now turn to a description of the great Eighteenth Dynasty temples, Karnak and Luxor, as they came to be modified by the Nineteenth Dynasty rulers.

Valley of the Queens: Tomb of Queen Nefertari
1 Entrance
2 First chamber
3 Colonnaded mortuary chamber

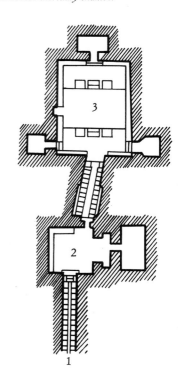

86. **Valley of the Queens: Tomb of Queen Nefertari, wife of Ramesses II (Nineteenth Dynasty).** This detail from the wall paintings shows the queen playing a board game somewhat like checkers.

Nineteenth Dynasty Karnak and Luxor

The construction of the great Hypostyle Hall in the Karnak temple is the work of Seti I and Ramesses II, the second and third rulers of the Nineteenth Dynasty. We have already mentioned that Horemheb had a pylon (the second) erected in place of the two last columns of Amenhotep III's colonnade. At that point, the north and south ends of the second and third pylons were connected by walls, which thus formed a vast rectangular space, divided in two at the center by Amenhotep III's colonnade. With the addition of seven rows of columns to the north and seven to the south, parallel to the two central rows, there was created a "forest" of 134 columns, with a central nave wider and taller than the lateral ones. This is the famous Hypostyle Hall that arouses so much admiration. The central columns (Amenhotep III's) are about twenty-two yards high and Ramesses II's columns are about fifteen with a diameter of over three yards; the distance that separates one from the other is too little to allow for effects of repetition or perspective. One interpretation is that these columns represent the overwhelming, crushing power of the pharaohs. If it is true that the architecture of Ramesses II tends toward the colossal, it is equally true that the Karnak Hypostyle Hall can be explained along other lines.

To begin with, an examination of the foundations has revealed that the columns had already been planned during the construction of the second pylon, built by Horemheb. In the second place, one of the most typical elements of the ancient Egyptian temple was the narrowing of space in approaching the interior; not only were the rooms and spaces smaller, but the ceiling became lower and the floor rose. There were probably mythological origins behind this device: remember that the sanctuary symbolized the primordial hill that emerged from the waters of chaos and served as the refuge of the creative god. And, indeed, the ancient Egyptians used the expression "go up" to the temple rather than "enter" the temple. From a practical point of view, the result was that every pylon added to a temple had to be larger than its predecessor, so that from outside the view of the whole complex came to be obstructed. Therefore, the dimensions of the Hypostyle Hall columns were especially conditioned by the proportions of the second and third pylons and by Amenhotep III's earlier colonnade. That the creation of such a gigantic structure was particularly congenial to the ambitious spirit of the Nineteenth Dynasty is a consideration, but it was not the only decisive element.

Ramesses II had many structures built at Karnak, but hardly any of them changed the plan of the temple proper. The relief decorations on Tuthmosis III's boundary wall and the additions to the obelisk sanctuary of the same pharaoh (east of the temple) deserve mention. And Ramesses II also made many additions at Luxor without, however, changing the arrangement of the sanctuary proper. In front of the pylon that closed off Amenhotep III's colonnade to the north, he had erected a vast arcaded courtyard with a double row of columns preceded by a high pylon. In the space between the arcade columns, huge statues of the king were erected. Other colossal statues were placed in front of the pylon, together with two obelisks (one of which eventually ended up in the Place de la Concorde in Paris in 1836).

88. Valley of the Queens: Another detail from the wall paintings in the tomb of Nefertari. It depicts the goddess Mut, kneeling at left, who protects the name of the queen with her wings, thus committing the queen to eternity; on the right, the goddess Selkis with the sacred sign of the scorpion on her head, is seated on the typical royal throne.

89. Valley of the Kings: Tomb of Prince
Amenherkhepeshef (Twentieth Dynasty).
In this detail from a wall painting, the
goddess Isis is embracing Ramesses III.

90. Valley of the Kings: Another detail from the wall paintings in the tomb of Prince Amenherkhepeshef shows the prince himself. Note the typical hairstyle of an Egyptian youth.

Other Nineteenth Dynasty Temples

In discussing the great cult and ceremonial temples of the Eighteenth Dynasty, we did not explore the mortuary temples of the kings because they have been so poorly preserved. Their outer stones were taken off to be used for new constructions, and their inner cores became submerged by the flood waters and later covered over by cultivated fields. Their poor condition was probably also due to the fact that the further away in time from the death of the king to whom these temples were dedicated, the more the cult tended to languish and then completely die. No pharaoh would be particularly interested in restoring the mortuary temple of one of his predecessors, and even less so in using the structures again, so that we have few remains of the Eighteenth Dynasty mortuary temples. However, it is known that the plan of these temples, in general, was not much different from that of Hatshepsut's temple at Deir el-Bahri; that is, it had terraces and arcaded courtyards.

In the Nineteenth Dynasty, however, the mortuary temple was patterned after the contemporaneous temples of the gods, with certain differences depending on the needs of the cult. Therefore we may speak about Nineteenth Dynasty temples in general, without making distinctions, at least in the description of the architectural elements, between the two types.

One of the best preserved temples of pharaonic Egypt is Seti I's funerary temple at Abydos, about three hundred miles south of Cairo on the west bank of the Nile. Abydos had been an extraordinarily important center at the beginning of pharaonic history, when it may even have been one of the capitals of the first two dynasties. Later it lost its political importance, but retained strong religious influence as the center of the Osiris cult. We have noted, too, how the rulers of the first dynasties most probably had two memorial tombs built, one at Sakkara and the other at Abydos. With the advent of the Fourth Dynasty, this custom died out and, as far as we know, the first pharaoh to build mortuary structures there again was Seti I, second pharaoh of the Nineteenth Dynasty. His temple is not that well known among average tourists since Abydos is far from the present-day tourist centers. Most probably it is for this reason that Abydos was spared the sacking that devasted the Thebes and Memphis monuments (including the other two funerary temples Seti I had built at West Thebes).

To enter Seti I's temple at Abydos, one passes through a pylon to the east, which leads to a courtyard with two wells. The back wall of the courtyard is faced with an arcade, accessible by means of a central ramp that leads directly to the door of a second courtyard, arranged like the first one. The back wall of this second courtyard, however, originally included seven doors that Ramesses II later walled up (except for the central one). The doors were there because the sanctuary consisted of seven similar adjacent chapels in the form of seven small hypostyle halls (whose walls were never built). The seven chapels were dedicated (from south to north) to Seti I, Ptah, Re-Harakhte, Amon-Re, Osiris, Isis, and Horus. Through a door at the end of the Osiris chapel, one could pass into a sort of apartment behind the seven chapels, consisting of two hypostyle halls and three more chapels oriented north-south and dedicated to Isis, to Seti I as Horus, and to Seti I as Osiris. What makes this temple plan characteristic is an annex to the southwest part of the temple proper, which included a sanctuary

91. Deir el-Medinet: Tomb of Sennedem (Nineteenth Dynasty). In this detail from the wall paintings, the god Anubis, with a dog's head, embalms the dead sovereign.

On the following pages:
92. Deir el-Medinet: Tomb of Pashedu (Twentieth Dynasty). In this detail from the wall paintings, the dead king, under a palm tree, drinks the water of regeneration.
93. Deir el-Medinet: Tomb of Pashedu. Another detail of the wall paintings shows the dead king's relatives. Note the attempt to differentiate the various generations by the color of their hair — white, gray, and black.

of the Memphite gods Ptah-Sokaris (connected to the mortuary ritual) and Nephthys (connected to the offering ritual). Finally, there was a sanctuary for the boat of Amon and several chambers used as storerooms or for other matters connected with the cult.

Seti I's son and successor, Ramesses II, also had a temple of the same type built at Abydos, a little north of his father's. Oriented north-south, it included a first pylon that gave access to a courtyard; both of these have been completely destroyed. On the eastern side of the courtyard, to the left of the entrance, there was a chapel built on a sort of pedestal reached by a step ramp. At the end of the courtyard there was a second pylon, followed by another courtyard whose north, east, and west sides were flanked by "Osiris" pillars (that is, representations of the king in the garb of Osiris). On the south side of this courtyard, three steps led to an arcade from which one gained entrance to a hypostyle hall, followed by another one of exactly the same dimensions, the rear wall of which opened on to a triple sanctuary.

Ramesses II's mortuary temple at West Thebes — often known as the Ramesseum — is a "must" for any tourist's itinerary. It is not

perfectly preserved, but the imposing aspect of its ruins never fails to impress even the most hurried visitor. Oriented east-west, and preceded by a pylon, it includes a courtyard, on the southern side of which was grafted the facade of a sort of palace with a colonnaded reception hall and a throne room. The facade, fronted by an arcade with double rows of columns, also had a window, the so-called "window-of-appearance": this was where the king presented himself to the exultant population. There then followed a second courtyard surrounded by an arcade and decorated with Osiris pillars. Three doors afforded access from this courtyard to the hypostyle hall, with naves wider than the three doors. The south door leads, through the hypostyle hall, to a sanctuary divided into three chapels, preceded by a hypostyle hall and a vestibule. The central door leads via the widest nave to the principal sanctuary of the temple, through two more hypostyle halls and a vestibule. Finally, the north door corresponds to similar rooms that lie open next to the great hypostyle. Unfortunately the back part of the temple is the worst preserved and not much can be said about the numerous rooms that surround the sanctuary; only the ground-plan of these rooms can be reconstructed. Probably the central one, the most important, was Amon's; the second was dedicated to Amon and Mut, according to some scholars, and to Seti I according to others.

Abu Simbel and Medinet Habu

After what was said at the outset about the unsurpassed stone-cutting skill of the ancient Egyptians, the *tour de force* realized by Ramesses II's architects at Abu Simbel in Nubia should come as no surprise. Yet it is understandable that these two sanctuaries — hewn out of the rock cliffs flanking the Nile at this point — continue to astonish visitors. Abu Simbel in recent years became the symbol of that part of Nubia submerged in the waters of the Nile as a result of the construction of the great Aswan Dam; the removal of the major parts of the monument to high ground is, in turn, one of the amazing achievements of modern technology. We shall, however, describe Abu Simbel as it was originally constructed in the rock cliffs bordering the Nile.

The largest of the two sanctuaries, dedicated to Ramesses II, was an ingenious transposition in rock of the common temple plan. In fact, the rocky cliff was cut on the outside in the form of a pylon; in front of this the four famous colossi representing the seated pharaoh, although cut out of the same rock, look much like those statues found in front of traditional temple entrances. The interior included a hall with a central nave flanked by Osiris pillars; this replaced the second courtyard of such temples as Ramesses II's mortuary temple. There then followed a hypostyle hall at the end of which were three chapels, the central one naturally being the largest and containing four statues of Ptah, Amon-Re, Ramesses I, and Re-Harakhte — all of this also hewn out of the natural rock of the cliff. The "minor" temple, dedicated to his wife, Nefertari, situated a little north of the first, had a simpler plan; a pillared hypostyle hall led to a vestibule that opened onto the sanctuary, dedicated to the goddess Hathor. The facade was decorated with colossal statues (about ten yards high) of Ramesses II and Queen Nefertari.

94. Deir el-Medinet: Tomb of Pashedu. In another detail from the wall paintings, the dead king receives the water of regeneration from the sycamore goddess.

The mortuary temple of Pharaoh Ramesses III, the second and greatest of the Twentieth Dynasty rulers, at Medinet Habu belongs to a later period. However, because of the analogies it presents with Ramesses II's funerary temple, it fits in perfectly with a discussion of Nineteenth Dynasty architecture, as it represents its last great phase. In fact, after the death of Ramesses III, the royal authority did not succeed in holding the nation in its power that much longer: Medinet Habu was, indeed, the last great architectural work in pharaonic Egypt. As in Ramesses II's temple, it was surrounded by a boundary wall that enclosed storerooms and houses for the priests. The principal gateway of the outer wall, aligned along the temple axis, looked like a small fortress with its two towers joined by a passage above the door. Passing through a vast courtyard and a pylon, one entered, through a second wall, another courtyard where the temple entrance was situated. This was composed of a pylon followed by a courtyard, whose north side was flanked by a row of Osiris pillars. The south side, as in the case of Ramesses II's temple, consisted of the facade of the palace decorated with a colonnaded portico, two doors and a window-of-appearance. The palace also had a reception hall and a throne room.

The western part of the courtyard contained a second smaller pylon that led into another courtyard bordered on the west by Osiris pillars, on the north and south by columns, and on the west by both pillars and columns. One then entered a hypostyle hall flanked to the north and south by little rooms. Then one passed into another hypostyle hall whose back wall had three doors — providing access to a third hypostyle hall — which corresponded to the three chapels that opened onto the back wall of this last hypostyle hall. The central sanctuary was the largest and was dedicated to Amon; the other two were dedicated to the gods Mut and Khonsu. Finally, to the rear there were two series of transverse chambers dedicated to various gods.

The Significance of Nineteenth Dynasty Temples

What can we learn from such a brief examination of the plans of the Nineteenth Dynasty temples? If we focus on the works of Ramesses II at Karnak and Luxor, the two greatest national sanctuaries, we will note one fact above all. Despite the grandiose nature of the constructions, they do not really impinge upon or modify the basic nucleus of the temple. We have already seen how the courtyard and the hypostyle hall constitute the least secret parts of the sanctuary, those open to the public. It is thus clear that the ruler's interest did not lie in the cult itself, but rather in developing those features that allowed for wider contact with many levels of the population. Obviously, in doing this, the pharaoh had to choose a means of expression that would be much more immediately accessible for the spectators. It is in this sense that we must interpret the grandness of the means employed and the importance given to the decorations that covered all the available surface space. It is in this sense, too, that we must interpret those "scenographic" effects found in architecture of the period. We are here seeing a real incursion, on the part of the royal personages, into the more properly religious territory of the sanctuary. In this, as we have said before, the kings of the Nineteenth Dynasty profited by the attitudes taken by their predecessors in the Eighteenth, and developing them to their logical conclusions.

However, it is also evident that Ramesses II was much less interested in Thebes as the center of the Amon cult than the Eighteenth Dynasty rulers had been. With the large-scale reorganization of the empire and the ever-growing importance of the middle class, the Amon priests saw their once prime function diminish. Thus, too, there were an infinite number of temples dedicated to various gods built and reconstructed during this period, and often in the most unexpected places. This had several effects. Besides helping to lessen the economic and political weight of the Amon priests and serving as a means of worship for those who did not live at Thebes, these temples rendered valuable service in helping the state in its administration, furnishing new bases for employment and for the control of local production. Meanwhile, the Nineteenth Dynasty kings had even moved their capital to Pi-Ramesses in the northeastern part of the Delta — one more instance of the Egyptian pharaohs' tradition of changing the capital to conform with a major reorientation of political policies.

In this new situation, the royal authority had to do everything to attract the attention of the people. And in a context of decentralization, in a society in which Thebes and Amon no longer constituted the unifying element, this energizing role was assumed by the pharaoh

95. Deir el-Medinet: Tomb of Inherkhaui (Twentieth Dynasty). In this scene from the wall paintings, a cat with rabbit's ears, connected with the sun mythology, kills Apopus, a serpent-god of the underworld.

97. Karnak: Sanctuary of Amon: This is a view of the northern side of the first courtyard, as seen from above the first pylon. This section was built in the Twenty-second Dynasty but bears traces of Nineteenth Dynasty architecture.

On the following pages:
96. Karnak: Sanctuary of Amon: The avenue of the sphinxes in front of the first pylon.

himself. By this time the pharaoh was everything in Egyptian life. The mortuary temples demonstrate this; Seti I's at Abydos, Ramesses II's at West Thebes, and Ramesses III's temple at Medinet Habu all have chapels dedicated to the cult of the pharaoh. This is shown particularly in the palace situated before the first courtyard of these temples. Amenhotep III had already built a residence next to his mortuary temple, but it was only with Ramesses II that a palace entered organically into the structure of the temple itself. And the festival. hall of Tuthmosis III at Karnak, which represented the first schism between royal cult and divine cult, found its most dramatic correlation in the Nineteenth and Twentieth Dynasties.

98. Karnak: Sanctuary of Amon. One of the sphinxes with the head of a ram (one of the sacred animals of the god Amon) protects the figure of the king; originally, the king probably represented Ramesses II, but later kings usurped the figure for themselves.

99. Karnak: In the first courtyard of the sanctuary of Amon, between the first and second pylons, stands this colossal statue of the Amon priest, Pinedem, who assumed royal powers during the Twenty-first Dynasty. It is possible that this statue originally represented Ramesses II and was then usurped by Pinedem.

All this is best demonstrated in the great temple of Abu Simbel, where everything — science, construction techniques, and even symbolic expression — was put at the service of the king. Because of its particular orientation and its proximity to the Tropic of Cancer, the rays of the sun penetrated directly into the sanctuary between January 10th and March 30th and between September 10th and November 30th every year, illuminating, according to the day, the statue of Amon, or Ramesses II, or Re-Harakhte (but never Ptah's, because he was not a solar divinity). It was by such devices, which some today might consider parlor tricks, that the king's policy was fully expressed. It tended to find, through its constant reference to Re (present, by design, in the very name of the king) motives for exaltation; so much so that, in more than one temple of this period, the pharaoh is hidden under the garb of Amon-Re.

Final Stage of the New Kingdom

For all the power and grandeur monopolized by these great pharaohs of the New Kingdom, we cannot ignore the role of the middle class in these developments. Near West Thebes , a village has been uncovered not far from Deir el-Medinet. Here lived the skilled workers employed in constructing the royal tombs and the notables' tombs. Besides the rich documentation it has given us of the inhabitants' daily life, this settlement has provided testimony of particular interest to us: the workers' own tombs, situated in the hills that overlook the village. Common, humble people who came from every part of Egypt, yet they could afford the luxury of preparing tombs of more than one room, decorated with paintings that reveal to us in a singular manner the tastes of the lower levels of society. Thus we see file past our eyes scenes and motifs clearly borrowed from those contained in the great Egyptian tomb paintings, and treated in a much freer way, with much attention given to popular elements and religious beliefs centered around the adoration of "good" gods, so to speak. The great divinities of the official religion came to interest the lower classes less and less; this was doubtless due to the strong decentralization previously described.

Finally, this phenomenon at West Thebes provides the first signs of a development that was to accelerate in the centuries following the death of Ramesses III (in 1166 B.C.). The central pharaonic authority had begun to lose its hold on all aspects of public life; the Egyptian people were becoming increasingly alienated from their country's destiny. This led, among other things, to the growth of magical practices and superstitions as a solution to the problems of daily life.

Strictly speaking, the New Kingdom is considered to have survived through the last of the Twentieth Dynasty kings, Ramesses XI, who died in 1085 B.C. But by this time the pharaohs had already lost their capacity to sustain major construction projects. The final blow was dealt by a profound economic crisis, due in part to the emergence of iron-using peoples in the eastern Mediterranean and the Near East. The balance of power in the ancient world was shifting. Symbolic of this was the tendency in Egypt itself for the nation's political life to concentrate in the Delta, where any monuments were especially vulnerable to the ravages of flood waters. Egypt, the "gift of the Nile," temporarily lost its special sense of identity and mission.

THE PTOLEMAIC PERIOD

The Ptolemies Rule Egypt

During the many centuries that followed the end of the New Kingdom, Egypt was weakened by both internal rivalries and external pressures, often being literally invaded and ruled by foreigners, including Assyrians and Persians. By the time Alexander the Great conquered Egypt in 332 B.C., the world had already changed profoundly. The Mediterranean basin had become the center of all political and economic life. The sea was dominated by Greece and Carthage; the power of Rome was beginning to take shape. Alexander's general, Ptolemy, ruled Egypt after Alexander's death in 323 B.C., and his successors, Macedonian-Greeks known as the Ptolemies, continued to rule Egypt for almost three centuries.

Ptolemaic Egypt was but one of the monarchies into which Alexander's empire had been divided. This is not the place to discuss the profound changes made in the ancient world's political system by these states; suffice it to say that each of these monarchies followed a policy of trying to make itself the leading country, each according to the particular social situation. Until Rome intervened and made the Mediterranean basin its dominion, these Hellenistic monarchies sought a new international balance of power. And this fundamental factor implies a second: the internal strengthening of the individual monarchies. Obviously, too, the Ptolemies would sooner or later attempt to strengthen their hold by exploiting the age-old tradition of Egyptian monuments. We shall examine the results shortly.

Meanwhile, we are particularly fortunate to possess considerable remains of Ptolemaic Egypt. The great number of papyrus documents, which the local climatic conditions have preserved, allow us to make a quite thorough social-economic reconstruction of the period, since these documents dealt with many aspects of official concerns and everyday life. Yet this good fortune is not without its negative side, as the existence of such a quantity of written documents has diminished the need for a study of the more strictly monumental remains. Added to this is the fact that the archaeological material of the period has so many ties with both classical and pharaonic culture that the Egyptologist is rarely equipped to study this period, since such a study requires an intimate knowledge of many different disciplines.

We can thus say that the Ptolemaic period in Egypt presents a unique situation in the study of the ancient world. We should also consider another phenomenon: the great quantity of documents preserved is not due only to the favorable climatic conditions; the other Hellenistic kingdom did not produce a proportionate amount of documents that were then lost over the years. In this sense, Egypt's Ptolemaic administration was an exception among its contemporaries, and this was due to the social situation in Egypt.

The basis of the Egyptian economy remained agriculture, and the Ptolemies understood that to reorganize the country it was first necessary to reorganize the agricultural system. The goals that inspired the new owners of the Nile Valley were different from those of the preceding dynasties. The pharaohs had been Egyptians, and they sought a balance of forces within their own country. The Asian empire founded in the Eighteenth Dynasty was in answer to particular national problems, and the entire pharaonic foreign policy was based almost exclusively on the idea of making Egypt autonomous. The Ptolemies, on the other hand, were Macedonian Greeks; their world was not in Africa but in Greece, or better yet, in that huge, more or less Hellenized community that composed Alexander's empire. This meant that they always kept their eyes on what was happening outside the Two Lands. And so it was that Egypt was no longer an end, but a means; as such, it was fairly well exploited. It was a question of taking the most profit possible from the country, with which the Ptolemies could maintain a pre-eminent position in the political world of the time.

In order to achieve this, it was necessary that the Ptolemies not allow any Egyptian resource to be wasted. Every single operation was planned and controlled from above in its most minute details. Once again the state took control of all the nation's activities. This gave rise to a new form of centralized state system. The structures and procedures were Greek, and these were applied to the Egyptian conditions. We must not forget, either, the social context that already existed when the Ptolemies took the pharaohs' place. By now we are well aware of how the ancient Egyptian state was organized, what importance the administrative-functionary class had, how all the resources and products of the land were gathered together by the central power to be redistributed at all levels. Even if the available documentation relevant to the last centuries preceding the Greek occupation does not provide that many details, we can safely assume that the administration of the country had not radically changed since the New Kingdom.

The Ptolemies, however, had a weapon at their disposal that, although introduced earlier in Egypt, had not yet exercised its maximum effect: this weapon was money. The use of money in Egypt allowed the introduction of a new system of tax-levying, the so-called contract system. Whoever had a certain amount of money at his disposal could obtain from the state the contract for the collection of taxes; that is to say, he bought from the government the right to collect the taxes

100. Philae: The capitals of the southwest corner columns to the kiosk of Trajan (2nd century A.D.). In the background can be seen the second pylon of the temple of Isis (Ptolemy XIII, 1st century B.C.). Ever since the construction of the old Aswan Dam, the island of Philae with its temples has been periodically inundated, but a project is now underway to make the monuments permanently accessible.

101. **Edfu: The Temple of Horus.** This is
the northern side of the courtyard, with
the entrance to the vestibule before the
hypostyle hall. The door was originally
flanked by two statues representing falcons,
the sacred animal of the god Horus, but
only one now remains.

102. **Edfu: Temple of Horus.** The statue
of the falcon, sacred animal of Horus, which
flanks the entrance to the vestibule.

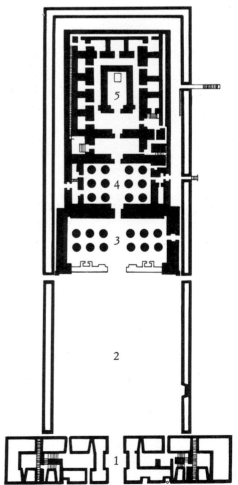

Edfu: The Temple of Horus
1 Entrance
2 Courtyard
3 Vestibule
4 Hypostyle hall
5 Sanctuary

from the people. This was the system already in use in Greece. The Ptolemies, however, grafted it onto the already existing Egyptian structures, making the contractors a intermediaries between the taxpayers and the official collectors, who belonged to the traditional state bureaucracy. Having thus resolved the most pressing problem of the state economy, the Ptolemies were able to dispense considerable amounts of money into other areas of their empire.

Another fundamental change that grew out of the Ptolemies' search for international prestige, was the need for a more modern, readily available army. Here they could not count on local elements. We have already observed that, since the death of Ramesses III, the Egyptian population began to experience a profound alienation from the destiny of the nation and public life. After several centuries during which no real authority emerged to win the loyalty of the people, Egyptians saw foreigners ascend the throne — first Libyans and Nubians, then the Assyrian and Persian occupations. Finally there occurred a great economic crisis, as a result of which the lower levels of the population could think of nothing more than earning their daily bread. Under such circumstances, no army composed of Egyptians would be very reliable. And so the Ptolemies used foreign troops, for the most part Greek mercenaries, to whom the Ptolemies were forced to grant considerable privileges in order to keep them bound to the government.

Alexandria and Egyptian Culture

Ptolemaic Egypt found its most illustrious symbol in the city of Alexandria, which, if not strictly speaking the capital of the country, was the residence of the new rulers. Presumably founded by Alexander during his brief sojourn in Egypt, at the western fringe of the Delta on the Mediterranean Sea, Alexandria soon became the depository of the new Hellenistic culture. Well aware of Alexandria's cultural and political importance, and above all of the "public relations" role it would play in the world of that time, the Ptolemies made sure that this city never became integrated with the rest of the country. It remained essentially Greek; not "in" Egypt, but "near" it. This is not the place to discuss the tremendous influence Alexandria had on its age; this is already well known and is part of Western history. But from the Egyptian point of view, the Alexandrian culture was almost exclusively Greek, in that it was the expression of the Greek ruling class and its policy, which was in turn directed toward the broader Hellenistic world. However, it is obvious that, although isolated and yearning for past glories, there must have existed in Egypt another official culture, that of the local ruling class. Inevitably the Ptolemies had to take this into account.

Unfortunately, the period preceding Alexander's arrival is not well-documented. The nation at that time was a satrapy — that is, one of the political-administrative entities, much like a provincial colony, that made up the Persian empire. We do not know to what extent the Persians intervened in the internal affairs of Egypt. It seems probable that they limited themselves to controlling the formal situation without changing its substance. Certainly the only strong and organized indigenous sector must have been the temple establishment, owning of vast amounts of land that allowed it to lead a fairly autonomous life.

Dendra: The Temple of Hathor
1 Entrance
2 Vestibule
3 Hypostyle hall
4 Sanctuary

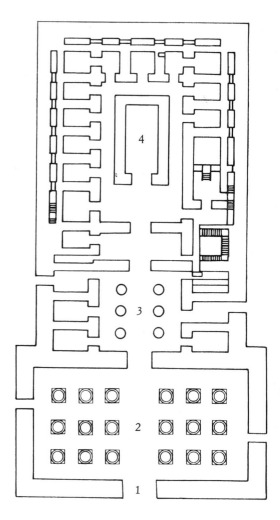

103. Edfu: The Temple of Horus. This is
the end of the southern wall of the birth
house, built by Ptolemy X (1st century
B.C.).

The most likely result was that the official Egyptian culture began to lose its secular character that was so typical of the periods when the country was governed by a homogeneous and organized central power. The temple came to represent a small minority that was no longer representative of the entire population. Moreover, difficult economic and political conditions, under which the lower classes had been living for some time, produced a general mistrust of the traditional structures. There developed the devotion to magical practices and beliefs in gods who were no longer tied to the royal mythology or to the traditional theology, gods who might intervene immediately in answer to prayers. The Egyptians felt less and less "at home" in their world, and sought consolation elsewhere.

That this process began quickly is indicated by the experience of the Twenty-sixth Dynasty, when the princes of Sais, in the Delta, between the seventh and sixth centuries B.C. (on the eve of the first Persian occupation) succeeded in reestablishing the royal presence in the country for more than a century, supporting itself primarily on trade with Greece. It was no accident that the formal culture of the period turned back to the past: the artists took the Old Kingdom as their model, its expressions, gestures, and the archaic texts.

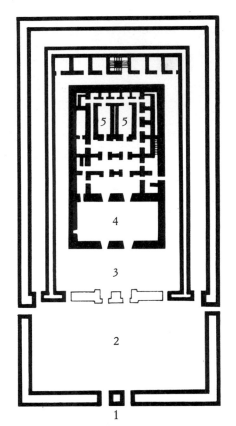

104. Kom Ombo: Temple of Haroeris and Sobek. This is the courtyard (left) as seen from the east, from in front of the pylon, now in ruins. To the rear are the columns of the vestibule. Note the originality of the plan, with its division into two parallel and equal parts.

105. Kom Ombo: Temple of Haroeris and Sobek, here seen from the southeast. From right to left: the first interior vestibule, the hypostyle hall, and the colonnaded vestibule (or exterior hypostyle hall).

Kom Ombo: The Temple of Haroeris and Sobek
1 Entrance
2 Courtyard
3 Vestibule
4 Hypostyle hall
5 Sanctuary

With the first Persian occupation in 525 B.C., the Egyptians must have lost every hope. It seems probable that the process of dissociation and alienation then began in earnest, and despite some short-lived successes between the first and second Persian occupation, the Egyptians were never again governed by one of their own countrymen. This was most important. For the Greeks, conquering Egypt did not mean defeating a nation but merely replacing previous foreign owners with new ones. It is clear that Alexander the Great was aiming at the Persian empire, and not at the title of pharaoh. He wanted to dismantle Persian power, and Egypt was one of its components. This is why during the early stage of their reign, the Ptolemies left the nation more or less in the same condition in which they found it.

However, when the Hellenistic monarchies began to maneuver for power in the ancient world, the situation changed radically. We have already indicated what steps they took to solve them. From an internal point of view — that is, the rulers' relations with the local population and culture — one aspect of the challenge remained: the Ptolemies could no longer appear as foreign occupiers provisionally in Egypt, but had to become sovereigns in the real sense of the word, permanently bound to Egypt's destiny. Alexander's successors became pharaohs. To achieve this, they needed access to the local culture.

106. Kom Ombo: In this detail from the wall reliefs of the vestibule of the temple of Haroeris and Sobek (left) we have a portrait of Ptolemy XIII (1st century B.C.).

107. Kom Ombo: In another detail from these vestibule reliefs, Ptolemy XII (1st century B.C.) is being crowned by the goddesses Nekhbet (patron of Upper Egypt) and Buto (patron of Lower Egypt), each wearing the crown associated with her region; note that the king wears both crowns.

This posed a delicate problem. There was certainly no thought of working toward complete integration of Greeks and Egyptians, as this would have meant above all the loss of the Ptolemies' "title" of Hellenistic monarchy, so decisive in the relationship with the other kingdoms. Furthermore, on the internal political level, this would have given the indigenous elements the chance to insert themselves in the higher administrative posts, with extremely dangerous consequences for the Ptolemies. It was therefore necessary to act on two different levels: Greek on the one hand, Egyptian on the other. We have seen how the former found expression in the city of Alexandria. The latter was manifested in a most tangible manner — by a series of temples.

The Ptolemaic Temples

Before examining specific temples, we should clarify one point. It is well known that in 30 B.C., as a result of the defeat of Mark Antony and Cleopatra's fleet by Octavian, Egypt became a Roman province. There then began a period of Egyptian history that presents a number of problems substantially different even from those of the Ptolemaic epoch. Given their complexity, we cannot consider these problems here. For various reasons, the Roman emperors continued to enlarge and decorate even the basic parts of the Ptolemaic temples, so that these monuments exist today as a complex of elements from different ages. Nevertheless, contrary to what we have noted with the pharaonic temples, the Ptolemaic-Roman temples present considerable unity. As a result, it is almost impossible to separate single elements from the total context of a Ptolemaic monument. However, our discussion must concentrate on the way the Ptolemies approached the temples, even when the Roman influence is quite strong.

Near the first cataract of the Nile (near present-day Aswan) there are several islands, the most famous of which is probably Philae. Even though ancient Egypt's territory extended further south the presence of the first cataract, rendered navigation impossible. Culturally and politically, the Aswan zone was Egypt's real southern border. From ancient times, Elephantine, an island just north of this cataract, had been the central junction for the Egyptian and the Nubian populations. This explains the series of sanctuaries at Philae (south of the cataract) which were dedicated to purely Nubian divinities, even if they are typically Egyptian in character and style.

But later, during the last centuries before the spread of Christianity, the goddess Isis enjoyed such popularity that her cult, extended far beyond Egypt. Sanctuaries dedicated to this goddess were constructed all over the Roman Empire. This success was principally due to the profoundly human qualities of the Osiris myth, which portrayed Isis as a loving and unhappy wife and mother. The Isis cult maintained its "home base" in Egypt where further important links with royalty still existed. Isis was considered to be the mother of the reigning pharaoh, and as such assumed a prominent role even in the official formulations.

To gain the recognition for the Ptolemies, and to reaffirm the religious basis of Greek and Roman royalty, a temple dedicated to Isis was constructed at Philae. Isis' temple at Philae, in the Ptolemaic-Roman version we know today, is the least unified yet most graceful complex of its kind; several of the Ptolemies had a hand in it. It included a pylon (Ptolemy XIII) preceded by a portico (Thirtieth Dynasty) and a courtyard; in a second courtyard the "birth house" (Ptolemy VII) was found; there followed a second pylon (Ptolemy XIII), which gave access to the hypostyle hall (Ptolemy VII) and then to the sanctuary (Ptolemy II). The birth house will be discussed later; for now, it need only be said that a myth and ritual are involved, not an actual birth.

(Philae and its temple, by the way, have been annually flooded ever since the construction of the old Aswan dam; with the new dam — although it is south of Philae — the island is permanently under water from the lake now formed by the old dam. But there is a plan to isolate the island and/or expose its temple.)

The temple dedicated to Horus at Edfu, on the west bank of the Nile about halfway between Aswan and Luxor, is much more organic and unified, as well as extraordinarily well preserved. By now we are

On the following pages:
108. Dendra: Temple of Hathor. This detail from the reliefs of the vestibule ceiling (across top of pages) depicts the signs of the Egyptian zodiac. The vestibule was constructed during the reign of the Roman emperor, Tiberius, in the 1st century A.D.
109. Dendra: Temple of Hathor: The temple facade (bottom left) as seen from the north.
110. Dendra: A close-up of one of the capitals in the vestibule of the Temple of Hathor. Note the feminine face with the ears of a cow, typical of the goddess.

well aware of the predominant influence Horus had on the pharaonic conception of royalty. Therefore it seems natural that such a remarkable temple should be dedicated to this god by the Ptolemies and that the clarity of its structural arrangement should correspond to the equally clear theological formulations about this god. You enter this temple from the south, through an imposing pylon (Ptolemy XIII) which affords access to a spacious courtyard (Ptolemy X) surrounded on three sides by columns. You then pass through a sort of external hypostyle hall, or colonnaded vestibule (Ptolemy VII), and then through a true hypostyle hall (Ptolemy IV) in order to reach the sanctuary (Ptolemy IV), which is preceded by two vestibules. The birth house (Ptolemy X) is situated outside the temple enclosure.

At Kom Ombo, between Aswan and Edfu on the east bank of the Nile, lies the temple consecrated to the gods Haroeris and Sobek. Although not well known, this temple is one of the most suggestive and interesting in Egypt, both because of its position, overlooking the river, and the originality of its plan. Basically it is similar to the Edfu temple, being formed of a pylon (Ptolemy XIII), forecourt (Augustus and Tiberius), vestibule (Ptolemy XIII), hypostyle hall (Ptolemy VII), three more vestibules (Ptolemy VI) and sanctuary (Ptolemy VI). However, since it is dedicated to two different gods, two equal, adjacent sanctuaries were built; two doors in each of the preceding structures correspond to these. There is a precedent for this in the seven chapels of Seti I's funerary temple at Abydos. But while

at Seti I's temple the division began only with the hypostyle hall, at Kom Ombo it continues from the sanctuary on to the outside. The birth house (Ptolemy VII) is outside the temple enclosure wall.

Even better preserved than the Edfu temple is the one dedicated to the goddess Hathor at Dendra, where the Nile curves after it passes Luxor. This temple as it stands today from the Roman age, and includes an enclosure wall that leaves a large open space in front of the entrance which consists of a colonnaded vestibule. There then follow the hypostyle hall, two vestibules, and the sanctuary. The birth house is outside the enclosure, as in the case of the previously mentioned temples. Elsewhere, only the Roman part of the temple at Esna (on the west bank of the Nile between Luxor and Edfu) remains, and this is a colonnaded vestibule.

Finally, the temple dedicated to the Nubian god Mandulis, at Kalabsha in Nubia, also belongs to the Roman age. During the construction of the high dam at Aswan, this temple was taken apart and reconstructed near Aswan, where its new desert home is called New Kalabsha. During the dismantling process, several older architectural elements, incorporated into the Roman structure, were discovered; these date back to an older Ptolemaic temple and to an even more ancient one constructed by Amenhotep II in the Eighteenth Dynasty. The present-day temple has a pylon, courtyard, colonnaded vestibule, hypostyle hall, and sanctuary. The birth house was situated southeast of the temple and was partially cut out of the rock in the hill on which the complex originally stood.

The Significance of Ptolemaic Temples

With the exception of Philae, all the temples we have so briefly described share a common element: their regularity, the "legibility" of the plan. In more than one case, the architects' search for harmonious relationships and the symmetry of the various parts, is quite

111. **Dendra: This is a detail (left) from the reliefs on the outer wall of the temple of Hathor. It depicts Queen Cleopatra VII, the famous Cleopatra of history and literature. (1st century B.C.)**

112. **Esna: Temple of Khnum. The temple facade (above) is here viewed from the northeast. It dates from the 1st century A.D.**

evident. A quick recollection of the Karnak complex will give a clear enough picture of the great difference in architectural intentions. But we cannot credit this simply to the influence of the Greeks in Egypt. A comparison with the fuller context of the pharaonic age temple would be more enlightening. We have stressed that the apparently chaotic arrangement of the Karnak complex met both the needs of the cult as well as the needs of the various religious and political policies pursued by the different pharaohs. The unity of the Ptolemaic temple, therefore, implies the cults' and the pharaohs' confidence in the underlying purposes. Essentially it is as if the ritual and mythological motivations behind the construction of all temples had been clearly defined by the outset of the Ptolemaic period.

The Ptolemies, in their reform work, also changed the state-clergy relationship by absorbing the land and possessions of the temple into the state administration. Not only was the autonomy of the temple restricted but a new source of profit was secured for the state. When it was later necessary to declare officially that the new sovereigns were descendants of the pharaohs, it was enough to restore, once again, the king-as-god doctrine, which made the king the focus of the daily worship in the temples. This took place in the first half of the third century

113. New Kalabsha: The Temple of Mandulis. This detail from the reliefs on the temple walls shows the god Mandulis, with a human head and hawk's body. It dates from the 1st century A.D.

EPITAPH OF TAIMHOTEP, WIFE OF A HIGH-PRIEST. (REIGN OF PTOLEMY XI)

O my brother, my spouse, my friend, O
    Chief-priest!
Let not your heart tire of drinking and eating,
of intoxication and of love!
Spend the day happy!
Follow your heart night and day,
do not trouble your heart.
What matter the years which are not spent
    on earth?
The West is the land of dream,
a deep darkness,
the abode of the dead:
sleeping is their occupation,
they do not awaken to see their brothers,
they cannot see their father or their mother;
their hearts forget their wife and their children.
The water of life which is the sustenance of
every living being is thirst for me:
it comes only to him who is on earth.
I thirst, even though water is at my side!
I do not know where I am now that I have
    arrived in this valley.
Give me fresh water;
say to me: "May you never be far from water."
I turn my face to the North-wind on the shore.
Surely my heart will be refreshed in its
    sorrow.
Death, whose name is "Come!", calls everyone
    to herself:
and they come directly to her, even though
    their hearts tremble with fear before her.
No man or god sees her:
the great are in her hand as well as the small,
no man can keep her away from his loved-ones:
she steals the little child from his mother more
willingly than the old man who is at death's
    door.
all those who are fearful pray to her,
but she does not turn her face to them.
She does not come to him who implores her,
she does not listen to him who praises her,
she does not look at what is offered to her.

114. **New Kalabsha: Another detail from the wall reliefs in the temple of Mandulis depicts the king in the attitude of prayer.**

B.C. According to the new arrangement between state and clergy, the latter drew from its income what was necessary for the ritual proceedings. We can then conclude that, to the extent that the king was head of the cult, he administered the temple funds. In this way, an even stronger form of control was established over the clergy's activity. This also permitted direct influence over the worship ritual. Thus the clergy found itself reduced to an organization serving as guarantor of the royal cult. Under these conditions, the priests found themselves deprived of that dynamic element that had once served as the catalyst for new policies. This had been clear even by the beginning of the Ptolemies' rule, and it is just this clarity that we find in the physical structures of the Ptolemaic temples.

A somewhat contrary process can be noted in the texts that appear on the Ptolemaic and Roman temple walls. Written in the traditional hieroglyphics, they reveal the extremely cerebral character the official Egyptian temple culture had arrived at during this period. The use of new signs, often created "on the spot," and of highly abstruse cryptographic writings, are indications of the ever-increasing distance that separated the official culture from the majority of the people. In certain respects, this could only favor the Ptolemies' policy; they certainly did not look favorably upon an alliance between the temple and the lower levels of society, as this would surely have caused an awakening of the nationalist consciousness.

One structure was especially typical of all the Ptolemaic temples: the birth house we have referred to previously. To understand it, we must first refer back to the myth of the divine birth of Queen Hatshepsut, painted on the walls of her funerary temple. Although other versions of this myth were employed at Luxor and Karnak by Amenhotep III and Ramesses II, it was in the Ptolemaic period that it was taken up again and developed. In fact, a separate structure was dedicated to the ritual of this myth, situated outside the enclosure of the typical Ptolemaic temple. Here there must have taken place a sort of sacred "birth," which represented the decisive moment of the divine birth. It is interesting to note that, if during the pharaonic age such a myth was linked with the more personal construction of the individual king, during the Ptolemaic period every temple complex had a birth house. We can thus consider the Ptolemaic birth house as the final flowering of the ancient Egyptian tradition that saw every pharaoh build his own temple alongside the complex dedicated to the divinity.

At the same time, a third form of culture was developing at the side of the official Greek and Egyptian cultures. In their efforts to introduce new methods of cultivation and new products to meet the demands of foreign trade, the Ptolemies encouraged colonists to come to Egypt. Many of the Greeks who came to the Nile Valley found themselves in more frequent and closer contact with the native population — and we are referring to people who lived far from large centers, in the rural areas. In this way, a popular type of culture developed, a culture that we do not see represented in the great official monuments of the age, but which with the passing of time was destined to spread more and more. This movement would culminate between the third and seventh centuries A.D. when Egypt, in its process of becoming Christian, tried to eliminate all links with its pharaonic past. The destroyers succeeded in the case of many of the figurative works of art — relief carvings, sculptured figures, wall paintings, and such. But the great monuments of ancient Egypt, many of which we have just explored, endured.

115. New Kalabsha: This is the temple of Mandulis, as seen from the southeast. Like many other monuments in Nubia threatened by the rising waters of the Nile after the construction of the high dam at Aswan, this temple was taken apart and reassembled in a new place. Here it is at the new location just south of Aswan, and thus is known as New Kalabsha to distinguish it from the original site in Nubia.

APPENDICES

THE EGYPTIAN MONUMENTS THROUGH THE AGES

Every discipline inevitably generates its own contradictions, and archaeology is no exception. One of the most dramatic paradoxes in archaeological research is inherent in the very process of excavation. Many people (and, unfortunately, even some archaeologists) seem to think that an archaeologist's job consists exclusively of excavating: the typical image is of a person armed with pick and shovel, intent on unearthing as many ancient remains as possible. This is as naive as saying that a doctor's work consists solely in dissecting corpses. In reality, the archaeologist is the person who, through a methodical and accurate examination of all the objects that have survived from a certain period (more specifically, those that show some trace of human activity) and bearing in mind all the other data at his disposal, tries to reconstruct a historical context for them. The digging operation, therefore, is only one phase of archaeological research, which is much more complicated and much less glamorous than the public generally realizes.

Suppose, for example, an archaeologist sets out to study Ramesses II's administrative policy. If he wants to verify how this policy was reflected, let us say, in the building activity on the period, the archaeologist would undoubtedly want to unearth an ancient Egyptian site of the period. Up to this point, nothing dramatic need have occurred. The "drama" begins to reveal itself when, in order to reach the layer of the site that corresponds to that pharaoh's epoch, this archaeologist has to remove the Islamic, Coptic, Roman, and Ptolemaic layers, one by one until he gets down to the remains of the Nineteenth Dynasty. Eventually, he may have to dig even deeper.

We may accept that all remains are useful to archaeological research, but it is much more useful to know how such remains were arranged at the moment of their discovery. We then arrive back at the aforementioned paradox: no sooner does the archaeologist unearth a historical remain, than he destroys it forever. This is the reason why excavation should be undertaken only when there are crucial reasons for doing so; this is also why a good archaeologist must be able at all times to reconstruct — by means of notes, plans, reliefs, and photos — if not physically, at least on paper, the context he has destroyed. A bad archaeologist is like a person who takes apart a very complicated apparatus in order to see "how it is made," without being able to put it together again. At the end, he will have a pile of screws, bolts, and pieces of various forms but they will be of no use. In other words, rather than dig badly, it is better not to dig at all.

We tend to equate ancient monuments with "ruins," with the implication that the more ruined they are, the more ancient. Yet with the majority of sites it is not time that ruins them, it is man. It is virtually certain that where fallen, dilapidated, and shattered buildings or statues are to be found, man has already been there. One of the few ancient cities that still provokes admiration for its fine state of preservation is Pompeii, and yet Carthage was much, much larger. The difference is that the outpour of Vesuvius passed over the former, whereas the Romans passed over the latter. All this is not recrimination; it is mere observation. One of the characteristics of human beings is to intervene incessantly in their environment. Which raises still another paradox: it is because man leaves his traces everywhere that the archaeologist can document the history of civilization.

Then there is another responsibility that archaeologists must assume with their work. In our time there prevails the principle that every monument must be restored as near as possible to the aspect and function for which it was destined when originally created. Naturally this is not a question of reconstructing the monument exactly as it was and where it was; rather, it means removing from the monument whatever was added over the centuries and which alters its original forms. An excellent idea, in our opinion; but it is often difficult to know what to remove and what to preserve. Certainly, if we think of Rome's Colosseum used as a rubbish depository, or the Parthenon used as a powder magazine, it is unlikely that anyone with the least bit of sensitivity would hesitate for a moment. On the other hand, who would feel inclined to demolish St. Mary of the Angels church in Rome in order to "save" the Diocletian Baths? Or destroy the Colosseum in order to restore the gardens of the Domus Aurea, Nero's "golden house"?

Obviously these particular instances are rather easy to resolve, but there are many problems of restoration whose solution would be extremely difficult. And here we come to the question of sensitivity or personal taste on the one hand and, on the other, the considerations of a particular period and society in which certain decisions regarding monuments are being made. We need only think of Sir Arthur Evans reconstructing the Minoan palace at Knossos, or of Mussolini destroying the Augusteum in order to unearth Augustus' mausoleum. We may conclude that the scientific attitude of the archaeologist is only one of the many attitudes man assumes with respect to the monuments erected by his fellow men.

The Royal Archaeologists of Ancient Egypt

All we have said so far applies to Egypt as well as to any other culture. We have seen, for instance, how the development of the Karnak complex was due mainly to a series of pharaonic interventions determined by changes in the general course of both religious affairs and the relationship between royalty and clergy. The Middle Kingdom sanctuary declined and finally disappeared altogether, and the chapels of Sesostris I and Amenemes I became the filling for the third pylon.

There is another remarkable and significant case of political "exploitation" of a famous Egyptian monument. Between the front paws of the Great Sphinx of Giza, there is a granite stele that bears a hieroglyphic inscription. In this text, King Tuthmosis IV of the Eighteenth Dynasty relates how, when still a young prince, he went hunting and grew tired, and then slept in the shade of the statue. The god Harmachis (one of the aspects of the sun god, with which some ancient Egyptians identified the divinity represented by the Sphinx) appeared to Tuthmosis in his dreams and promised him the throne of Egypt, provided that he free his statue's body from the sand that covered him. Now we know that during the Eighteenth Dynasty at least, the kings sent the crown prince to Memphis to prepare him for his future responsibility as ruler. If this indicates the cultural importance of the Lower Egypt city, it is also expresses the constant link sought by the rulers of this dynasty with the sun cult, which had its center at Heliopolis, not far from Memphis. Evidently Tuthmosis IV wanted to demonstrate his devotion to Harmachis and so added the stele to that most prominent place. He was also responsible for another bit of restoration when he had that single obelisk built in the place that had been chosen for it by Tuthmosis III; the importance of this obelisk, now in Rome, has already been discussed.

The reign of Ramesses II was a period of great changes and renovations: it is difficult to find a pharaonic monument in Egypt today that does not bear his mark somewhere. This activity of Ramesses II was an integral part of his intention to make the figure of the pharaoh the only reference point in the nation's culture. His practice of "usurpation" is typical in this regard.

We are by now familiar with the idea that in ancient Egypt representing or writing something was like making it live. Therefore, all the Egyptian statues that portray a person have an inscription with that person's name, followed by a detailed list of his titles and the posts he held — that is, all the information that could help to define this person. It follows that whoever wanted to make a "portrait" his, would only need to rub out the inscription and put another one in its place with his name, titles, and so on. This phenomenon is often to be found throughout pharaonic history, but it takes on grand proportions during Ramesses II's epoch. For example, it seems that the colossal statues bearing his name, set between the columns of the Luxor temple courtyard, are really statues of Amenhotep III that Ramesses II usurped.

Some interesting documentation belonging to the Nineteenth Dynasty was brought to light in King Djoser's funerary complex at Sakkara. During excavations there, some writing in ink was discovered on various places along the walls, writings that testified to the admiration Nineteenth Dynasty visitors had for this great monument of the Third Dynasty. These are among the first examples of that mania (still in vogue today) of writing one's name on famous monuments. In this case, the signatures have contributed enormously to solving the problem of dating this monument at Sakkara. Actually, before commencing excavation here, Egyptologists believed that the oldest Egyptian architectural monuments were the Giza pyramids. When the Sakkara complex was unearthed, not all the scholars were able to place it in the right period, as it seemed impossible for such structures to have preceded the building of the Great Pyramids, especially since the former adopted models and followed architectural "rhythms" hitherto not found in Egypt. Thus many early scholars elaborated the theory that this was an ancient monument that had been "retouched" by the Greeks much later. Today we know that the Djoser columns, however "un-Egyptian" they may be, certainly have nothing to do with classical Greek temples. The decisive factor in settling this question was exactly those signatures of Nineteenth Dynasty visitors. These automatically excluded any possibility of the monuments being Greek, since the Greeks did not arrive in Egypt until six hundred years later.

Another rather exceptional piece of pharaonic archaeological documentation is a series of papyrus documents concerning an investigation into the violation of tombs. The investigation was conducted in the Theban zone under Ramesses IX of the Twentieth Dynasty. It seems obvious that the royal tombs could not remain inviolate for long. As far back as the First Intermediate Period, there is a rather pessimistic text that describes the various acts of "wickedness" committed in the temples because of a lack of stable authority, and among the acts listed was the violation of tombs. Tomb robbery probably never completely ceased, but during the late Twentieth Dynasty, when the state was in the midst of a great economic crisis, often the only way to keep alive was by stealing the treasures of the royal tombs. We know, from these papyrus texts, the names of some of these thieves, and we can often find links with persons of a much higher rank than common thieves; evidently corruption had by that time invaded all levels of life. There was then an attempt to save at least the pharaoh's mummies, by taking them from one hiding place to another. As far as we know, only the tomb of Tutankhamon was spared, as it had the good fortune of being hidden by the hovels of workmen who were constructing a necropolis for Ramesses VI. The archaeologist Howard Carter, after years of research, decided to remove these hovels and thus discovered the famous tomb in 1922; this decision is one of the most significant examples of the responsibility an archaeologist must sometimes assume.

One of the most interesting periods in pharaonic history was undoubtedly the time when Egypt was ruled by the princes of Sais, a city in the Delta. They represented the last dynasty of true Egyptians (the Twenty-sixth), and tried to raise the nation to the height of its former glory. From a cultural point of view, this period is characterized by serious study of the artistic forms of the past, especially of the Old Kingdom; this is commonly called the "Saitic Renaissance." And just as in the Italian Renaissance painters crawled on all fours into the "grottos" of the Oppian Hill (that is, the rooms of Nero's Domus Aurea, which had filled up with earth almost to the ceilings) in order to study the paintings there, so the Saitic artists went into the subterranean chambers of the Sakkara Step Pyramid to analyze the reliefs. Some of these Saitic artists' "tools" have been preserved, one of which was a squaring system used on the reliefs in order to study the artistic rules of the Old Kingdom.

Also from the Saitic period are the inscriptions of the Greek mercenaries on the colossi of the great Abu Simbel temple. We know that the rulers of the Twenty-sixth Dynasty had friendly relations with Greeks and favored trade relations between Egypt and Greece, setting aside a city, Naukratis, for the Greek merchants; Naukratis, was a commercial emporium situated in the western branch of the Delta, near Sais. Moreover, these Egyptian rulers used Greek mercenaries for their military expeditions. To that extent, the inscriptions come as no surprise. Yet it must have been quite an experience for these Greeks to find themselves so far from their homeland and in the presence of monuments totally foreign to their expression and way of life. Their inscriptions also happen to represent one of the oldest known set of documents in the Greek alphabet.

Egypt's Monuments Usurped by Foreigners

Among the many treasures from the Ptolemaic and Roman periods — specifically, in the form of papyrus letters and receipts — a large number have survived from the Theban zone. We are thus especially well informed about the situation of the monuments of this area, especially West Thebes. We have already noted that this was a unique case of a concentration of people who worked in connection with the local funerary activities. Political motives must have been the reason for such a concentration. Amenhotep III had already had a palace built near his mortuary temple (of which only the Colossi of Memnon remain), and we have seen how this was the place where the king met his people.

West Thebes thus developed into more than a "city of the dead"; it became a meeting ground between the king and his people. This is also demonstrated by the palaces annexed to the Nineteenth and Twentieth Dynasty royal mortuary temples. Given these conditions, it is obvious to expect West Thebes to become the center of the unofficial religion of the country, the one not connected with Amon. We may recall the local cults at Deir el-Medinet, the workers' village. Likewise, Amenhotep, Son of Hapu, prime minister of Amenhotep III, was granted the privilege of having his mortuary temple erected in this area.

We can surmise from the previously mentioned investigation into tomb violations that there were certain conflicts between the administrators of the east and west banks of the Nile at Thebes, indicating the distrust shown by those connected with the Amon clergy toward those on the opposite side of the river. Evidence of the tendency to take the law into one's own hands, so to speak, without appealing to the authorities, is given by the local cults at Deir el-Medinet and by the gradual increase of appeals made to the oracle in controversies during the Twentieth Dynasty. Moreover, we know that the workers of Deir el-Medinet organized strikes when they were not paid, and for this purpose they met in the little temple next to their village.

During the Ptolemaic period, West Thebes must have come to represent a center of religious rather than political importance; certainly the Ptolemies feared the influence of the Amon clergy. In the Luxor and Karnak temples, the Ptolemies replaced the two Eighteenth Dynasty sanctuaries, thus breaking with the traditional respect observed by the Pharaohs for over a thousand years. In 88 B.C. Thebes was the center of a rebellion, which was crushed by the Macedonians but during which many parts of the temples were destroyed. Probably the Amon clergy formed the last nucleus that could serve as a center for the rehabilitation of the Egyptian ruling-class culture — that is, a nationalistic reaction against foreign dominion.

At West Thebes, the damage was minor. Above all, the Ptolemies played on the rivalry between the "two Thebes," probably separating the two administrations. We see once again the policy of minimizing any agreement or union between the Egyptian ruling class and the lower classes, which could have been dangerous to the Ptolemies. On the other hand, West Thebes, being the center of the lower classes, was easier to control; it was enough to keep the people under the pressure of everyday activities so that they would have no chance of organizing themselves.

There thus began the mummy "boom." The fame of the Theban necropolis, the quantity of tombs it contained, and, above all, the mortuary temples so closely connected with popular cults, caused a great demand for tombs even before the Ptolemaic occupation. Meanwhile, the mummification of corpses — at first reserved exclusively for pharaohs, then slowly extended to include the cadavers of nobles and functionaries, and finally lower-class people — began to reach a point where it was no longer a religious rite, but an industry. The technique of mummification had already begun to show signs of decadence. As often happens, the more widespread a practice, the more hasty and inaccurate it becomes. Add to this picture the terrible oppression that taxes represented for the lower classes, and we will understand why they took the little money they had saved and used it to have a dead relative mummified. This is typical of the hope for a better future for those who are desperate in this life. No one wants to be miserable, least of all through eternity.

All this favored the formation of groups of persons who lived exclusively off funerary activity. There were "private" priests who carried out the religious rites, paid by their clients; there were also the embalmers. But this situation led to another development. Although the Theban necropolis was large, eventually there was a shortage of space. Naturally they could dig new tombs in the desert; but at that time, few persons had the means to do this. Thus they began using the more ancient tombs. Tombs that had been violated centuries before, or those forgotten by the deceased's relations, served the occasion perfectly; one needed only to locate them, put them in order, and remove the remains of the ancient owners in order to make a place for the new ones. Then, after paying the priest and the embalmer, it was necessary to pay those who found the tombs. And so the mummy trade was created, with its entrepreneurs, its boatmen who took the bodies across the Nile, and its storehouses where the mummies lay until a place could be found for them. The old mummies ended up being valuable commercial objects; they often represented the only wealth a family possessed, and a mummy was sometimes kept in the house, as a good-luck sign or as a sort of protective divinity. And this was not all: mummies were often used as a guarantee of payment; mortgages were negotiated with them.

This was the situation in which masses of Egyptians found themselves in this late phase of their history, when they were ruled by foreigners. As far as the monuments are concerned, it is futile to try to explain what effect such phenomena had on them, especially the pharaonic age tombs. We are better informed when it comes to the opinion the Greek and Roman visitors had of the Egyptian people; yet obviously they could not understand the situation for two basic reasons. The first is that they found certain practices absolutely inconceivable. And second, they were on the other side of the fence; they were the conquerors. He who dominates a foreign land inevitably feels the need to justify in his own eyes the reason why he has become a ruler, and he will expect from foreigners what he would never dare to ask from his own countrymen. It is far too easy to demonstrate hypocritically how those under one's domination are incapable of governing themselves and thus how they must be "civilized." And the Egyptians, with their traditions centered around their dead, certainly furnished their new rulers with material for such a line of reasoning. The "stranger" the things they did, the more justified the foreigners felt their presence to be.

As for the great West Thebes sanctuaries, we know for certain that the temple of Ramesses III at Medinet Habu, and that of Ramesses II, were turned into citadels of sorts. Evidently the storerooms and boundary walls must have still been standing, and during difficult times the population used them as refuges. Hatshepsut's sanctuary at Deir el-Bahri enjoyed a different destiny: it not only continued to function, but housed a new cult, that of Imhotep (Djoser's architect, identified by the Greeks with their Aesculapius, patron of medicine) and Amenhotep, Son of Hapu. Possibly this indicates an attempt on the part of the Greeks to introduce their gods in the popular Egyptian beliefs. Certainly the popularity of these new divinities was due to the fact that they were "healing" gods that the poor people could appeal to in time of need.

We should also mention the unique case of the Colossi of Memnon. In Homer's *Iliad*, Memnon, an Ethiopian hero, son of Aurora, went with his troops to the aid of Troy, and was tragically killed by Achilles. At first Ethiopia had no definite location in the minds of the Greeks; some held it was in Asia, others in Africa; at a certain point, the latter idea dominated. At the same time the first Greek visitors to Egypt sought a name to give to the builder of all those grandiose monuments whose meaning escaped them. Perhaps from the similar sounds of the name Memnon and the various corruptions of the names of such pharaohs as Amenemes I (Twelfth Dynasty) or Amenhotep III (Eighteenth Dynasty) — whose effigies these statues actually were — the Greeks ended up attributing these monuments to that legendary Memnon.

It so happened that when, after an earthquake, the upper part of the northern colossus of Memnon fell and was broken, the statue became the center of a curious phenomenon: at dawn it emitted a sound that was described by those who heard it as that of a lyre string snapping and breaking (This has been explained by the presence of crystals in the quartz rock the statue was made of; these crystals in some way adapted to the considerable difference in temperature in that area between night and day.) This occurred during Augustus' reign in the first century B.C., and the Roman conquerors, steeped in Greek culture, saw in the statue the famous Memnon who greeted his mother at the rising of the sun. The entire lower part of the statue is covered with inscriptions in Latin and Greek, written by visitors who rushed to the spot to witness the event. Even the Emperor Hadrian did not miss the spectacle, and the cultural pilgrimage reached its peak during his reign. Early in the third century A.D., the Romans restored the statue and in so doing ended the phenomenon.

The royal tombs in the Valley of the Kings, meanwhile, had been enjoying great "touristic" success. Romans, and above all Greeks, went to visit this valley, in much the same way we take guided tours today, often leaving their names on the ancient wall paintings and various comments on the monuments. As for Luxor, certainly in Diocletian's time a *castrum* — that is, a camp for the Roman legionaries — was installed in the temple area; the remains of this can still be seen, especially in the space between the temple and the Nile. What had been the "boat chapel" was walled up and used as a temple for the same legionaries. (In the nineteenth century, an English visitor succeeded in copying the paintings the Romans had walled over.) The name Luxor, in Arabic *el-Uxor*,

is nothing more than the plural of *qasr*, Arabic for "castle," which in turn represents the Arab corruption of the Latin *castrum*. So that Luxor corresponds to *castra*, or "castles," probably in reference to the fortifications that resulted from the changes made by the Romans to the temple.

With the spread of Christianity in Egypt, the Copts, the Egyptian Christian population, further damaged the pharaonic monuments. It is even possible that in the early Christian period, when there were struggles between pagans and Christians, some ancient temples were partially destroyed. Certainly the Copts wanted to avoid contact with the preceding culture and could not accept pagan structures as such. Once more Hatshepsut's temple was used, this time as a convent, while the temple at Medinet Habu housed a church. The phenomenon of monasticism that took hold among Egyptian Christians is better documented. The Thebans, especially, saw their monks remove themselves from inhabited regions for isolation and meditation; in this way spread the custom of using ancient stone caves or tombs as habitations. In some cases the monks were literally pitiless in mutilating the ancient paintings. Practically every pharaonic tomb bears traces of these monks.

The Monuments in the Shadows

And so, little by little, the memory of ancient Egypt weakened in the consciousness of people increasingly dominated by classical culture. With the Arab occupation of Egypt and the spread of Islam that began in the seventh century of our era, the pharaonic past was to be found only in the descriptions of classical authors. For several centuries to come, no European, as far as is known, succeeded in visiting the Nile Valley; therefore we have little information about the Arab period that corresponds to Europe's Middle Ages. Evidently all the most important pharaonic remains had fallen into disuse and had been more or less buried in the sand or had deteriorated. It is probable that they no longer interested the new conquerors, as they were merely souvenirs of a distant past that did not mean anything to them. It is not surprising, then, that Arab sources speak about them so little, especially those in Upper Egypt.

There was one exception: the Great Pyramids of Giza. The new Islamic capital, Cairo, grew up not far from ancient Memphis. This is one of the major causes of the loss of the Memphis remains as well as of the Memphis necropolis. The stone found there was removed and used for the construction of the new capital. It is not rare, even today, to find blocks of stone from the ancient center, some with inscriptions, forming part of a building in Cairo. This was also the reason for the loss of almost all the mortuary temples (Chephren's Valley Temple was spared because it was covered by sand) and the facing stones of the pyramids. However, the three pyramids of Giza remained to attract attention and, above all, to cause perplexity as to their possible origin. According to a tradition cited by more than one Arab source, in A.D. 820 the Caliph El-Mamoun wanted to take apart a pyramid to see what it contained. Told that this was impossible, he ordered that one be opened, the pyramid of Cheops. This is probably the origin of the opening that even today affords access to the monument. Inside the Mohammedans found a sum of money equal to what the Caliph had spent in having the pyramid opened. Another source, however, speaks of a chamber situated inside the pyramid containing a green "statue," covered by golden armor studded with precious stones. This story might symbolize the finding of Cheops' mummy, but we have no means of ascertaining its truth. Nonetheless, it is not impossible that the Caliph really did open the Great Pyramid.

Another interesting bit of information reported by various Arab historians is that the pyramids were completely covered with inscriptions. Now we have noted that the royal tombs of the Fourth Dynasty had none. It is thus assumed that the inscriptions in question were engraved by visitors. This was done at the Colossi of Memnon, at Abu Simbel, on the paintings in the Valley of the Kings, and at the Djoser complex at Sakkara. So it is unthinkable that the Cheops pyramid would not have them, for such a famous and great monument would certainly not have escaped the notice of monument signers. Probably there were many inscriptions that have since disappeared, but today the pyramid is full of signatures, even those of famous persons; the oldest belongs to Aibeck, founder of the Mameluke Bahariti dynasty, who lived around A.D. 1250. We can thus consider this date as the reference point for the removal of the pyramid facing. In fact, we know from an Arab historian, Abdel Latif, that the famous Saladin, Sultan of Egypt, had demolished several small pyramids in order to construct the Cairo citadel with their stones, at the end of the twelfth century A.D

During the Crusades, several European pilgrims succeeded in entering Egypt and in seeing the pyramids. These visits fit in perfectly with the preconceptions of these first Western "tourists," who, after having reached the Holy Land, liked to retrace the way of the Exodus from Egypt, arriving at Cairo after a long and tiring journey across Sinai. For these people, what was important in Egypt was connected to the Scriptures. During the entire Middle Ages, the Giza pyramids were interpreted as the granaries built by Joseph to make provisions for the great famine that was to devastate the Nile Valley.

An interesting piece of testimony concerning the exploitation of the Cheops pyramid's facing stones is given by the Baron D'Anglure, a Frenchman who visited Giza at the end of the fourteenth century. He narrates how he witnessed workers taking apart the facing by using levers on the blocks and then letting them fall to the earth. Moreover he says he was told that the greater part of Cairo monuments had been built with these stones, and that this operation had been going on for over a thousand years. Finally, the Baron notes that the pyramids were so huge that only the sound of the falling blocks and the workers gave any indication of what was being done, as both block and workers were so high up they were invisible.

We begin to encounter many Western sources in the fifteenth and, particularly, the sixteenth centuries, when the pilgrims were joined by merchants. The frontiers of the Orient were opened to European merchants at the beginning of the sixteenth century, and the first European ambassadors began to install themselves in Egypt on a permanent basis. This was accompanied by an increase in the number of publications with accounts of journeys to eastern lands, and the taste for the foreign spread among cultivated Europeans. A visit to the pyramids was an adventure that might be dangerous, as there was the risk of being attacked by Bedouins. Despite this, many Europeans went there and then published accounts of their experiences. Among other things, we owe to these hardy adventurers the report of one of the first cases of "tourist exploitation," on the part of the inhabitants of Giza. Although the Great Pyramid had been open for some time, the natives regularly blocked the entrance after every visit, in order to be able to "open" it up again for the next visitors and thus get a tip. At the end of the sixteenth century, Sakkara was added to the itinerary; the visitors liked to enter the mastabas and unearth the mummies in order to open them up and look for jewels.

As relations between Egypt and Europe increased in the sixteenth century, so did the Europeans' taste for the exotic; collecting became fashionable. Not only pilgrims and merchants went to Egypt, but also diplomats, missionaries, and adventurers, often "armed" with credentials and official jobs from their governments. The new breed of travelers was no longer content to visit the various places, but began to search for ancient manuscripts, especially Coptic and Arab ones. "Mummy powder" also came to be used in Europe for its "therapeutic" value. The traffic created by this product contributed to the destruction of the Sakkara tombs. And then the discovery in the tombs of amulets in the form of scarabs, the sacred beetles, was the basis for the fashion that has persisted up to this day.

The seventeenth century marked the beginning of interest in other places besides Sakkara and Giza. A visit to Upper Egypt could be dangerous, but there were some who took this risk. In 1668 two French Capuchin friars stationed in Cairo, Father Protais and Father François, penetrated Upper Egypt and described the ruins of Luxor and Karnak; however, they failed to connect these remains to Thebes, whose location had long been forgotten. Another of the early Europeans to try his luck was Father Vansleb, a German sent by Louis XIV's chief minister, Colbert. Vansleb was commissioned to reach Ethiopia and collect manuscripts in Egypt. The attempt failed, but it is certain that he at least reached the area near Tell el-Amarna. Then in 1692, Benoit de Maillet was appointed French consul in Egypt, and in his sixteen

years of service there he not only explored Cheops' Great Pyramid and made other important discoveries but also was the first to propose a plan for a scientific exploration of Egypt.

In the first quarter of the eighteenth century another French priest, Claude Sicard, described the ruins of Karnak and Luxor and became the first to identify them as the remains of Thebes. He visited the west bank of the Nile there, and thus saw the Colossi of Memnon and the colossal statue of Ramesses II at his mortuary temple (a statue now completely fragmented). He also succeeded in visiting about ten tombs in the Valley of the Kings, five of which were half ruined. And in 1721 he reached Aswan. Sicard was, in certain respects, the father of modern archaeology in Egypt.

From then on the road to the principal localities in Upper Egypt was opened. In 1731 the Frenchman Dr. Granger discovered the temple of Seti I at Abydos and the Ptolemaic temple at Edfu. Between 1737–1742 the Englishman Richard Pococke traveled in Egypt, going as far as Aswan. In 1737 the Dane Frederick Norden followed the course of the Nile past Aswan, and reached Derr, in Nubia. At the end of the eighteenth century Egypt was no longer a mysterious, obscure land to Europeans. Yet in this period there was a considerable decline in Egyptian-European relations, particularly commercial. The Turkish administration (dating back to 1517) was no longer able to maintain order in the country, and thus Egypt was at the mercy of a military caste, the Mamelukes. The native population lived in extreme poverty, and decreased in numbers. These were the conditions in Egypt when it was drawn into the modern world by Napoleon's French expedition.

The Dawn of Modern Archaeology in Egypt

The arrival of Bonaparte's troops in 1798 (accompanied by 175 artists, scholars, and scientists intent on studying the varied aspects of the country) signaled a real turning point in our knowledge of the pharaonic monuments. The amount of material discovered by the *Commission des Sciences et Arts* between 1798 and 1801, and published in the monumental *Description de l'Egypte*, constitutes to this day a precious source of information for the scholar, in particular because of the many monuments the French saw and described that no longer exist. A worthy product of French encyclopaedism, this *Description* inaugurated the scientific attitude toward pharaonic antiquities. We can thus consider this inventory of Egyptological material the starting point for the archaeological explorations of the last century and of this one.

It is impossible to give even a summary of the contents and results of this publication. What is important is to observe that it recorded the remains for the first time directly and objectively, reproducing exactly what the scholars saw. The proportions and measurements given to the monuments, and especially to the hieroglyphic signs in the illustrations that accompany the text, replaced the classical, Western style so typical of all preceding illustrations. Moreover, the volumes of this publication are full of dissertations that maintain an almost excessively rational distance from their subject. We no longer find mere visitors' impressions, often smacking of anecdotes or fantastic legends, but discourses based on logical considerations that arise from observation and concrete facts.

The publication of the *Description* between 1809 and 1828 had an enormous effect all over Europe. For one thing, the non-specialist could finally get a clear idea of the monuments he had heard so much about. Moreover, a great quantity of material was now made available to scholars, material that had either remained unknown or was inaccessible because of the difficulties and expense of a trip to Egypt. We must remember that the museums at that time were really little more than private collections, and thus were not only inaccessible to the public, but often had no material on Egypt. The only pharaonic objects one could see had been found in Europe itself, where they had been brought during the Roman Empire when certain eastern cults, especially that of Isis, were widespread even outside the Nile Valley. Therefore anyone who wanted to understand the pharaonic world had very little hope — unless his name happened to be Jean-François Champollion.

Before speaking of this exceptional scholar, it would be useful to say something about the famous Egyptian hieroglyphs. Hieroglyphic writing had been inscribed on the monuments of the very first dynasties; it was used for over three thousand years. Its most evident characteristic are the recognizable figures of persons, animals, and objects; in fact, most of these "pictures" were used much as we use the signs of our own alphabet — to indicate a specific sound. This script is, however, complicated by the fact that not all the signs have the same value; some of them indicate simple sounds while others indicate syllables; some are ideographs (symbols of an object or idea but with no value as sounds); and then others are not read from a phonetic point of view but rather serve as auxiliaries in the reading — that is, they "determine" the meaning of words. Besides the so-called monumental hieroglyphics, two more types of writing were used in ancient Egypt, the hieratic and the demotic. Both were cursive variants of the hieroglyphic — that is, more rounded, less detailed, and like our handwriting; they were used mainly in papyrus texts. With Egypt's occupation by the Ptolemaic Greeks, the Greek alphabet supplanted the local forms of writing, but this substitution depended on the introduction of the Greek language in official writings. And as the Greek alphabet and Greek language displaced Egyptian, an Egyptian who studied to become a scribe had to learn to read and write in Greek, even though he continued to speak Egyptian.

With the conversion of Egypt to Christianity the problem of the sacred texts arose. By this time, any Egyptian who could read and write did so in Greek. This — together with the tendency for the Christian doctrine to spread among the illiterate lower classes who spoke Egyptian — led to a compromise; Egyptian began to be written once more, but with the Greek alphabet. This new form of Egyptian came to be called Coptic, and it became the language of the Christians in Egypt. In the seventh century A.D. Mohammedan Arabs conquered the land and Islamism quickly spread to all levels of society; this brought about an Arab Egypt, whose inhabitants, Christians and Moslem, spoke and wrote Arabic. Coptic remained in use only for Christian worship services. This is more or less the situation in present-day Egypt.

The French under Napoleon, during the

course of some military construction near Rosetta, a village in the Delta, discovered a basalt tablet bearing an inscription in three different types of writing: Greek, hieroglyphic, and demotic. (After the defeat of the French forces in Egypt in 1801, "the Rosetta stone" was taken by the English; today it can be found in the British Museum in London.) The publication of the *Description*, as mentioned, gave great impetus to the resumption of Egyptological studies, above all to the attempt to decipher the hieroglyphic texts. Up to then, this had proved impossible because scholars thought hieroglyphics were only ideographs. Furthermore, they did not know the Egyptian language, so that even had the scholars succeeded in "sounding" the texts correctly, they would have been unable to translate and interpret them. Even the Rosetta Stone did not automatically solve the problem. Scholars assumed correctly that the three forms of writing contained the same text, but this was not enough to decipher the Egyptian language in detail. It was here that the figure of Champollion emerged in all his greatness.

Born in France in 1790, Champollion, even as a child, dreamt of deciphering the hieroglyphic signs. He began to study assiduously in order to learn all he could about ancient Egypt and Coptic Egypt. By the time he was twenty-one, Champollion was already a professor at the University of Grenoble and when copies of the Rosetta Stone inscriptions appeared in France, he was among the many scholars who examined them. Although various other European scholars made contributions — particularly the English physician, Thomas Young — it was Champollion who persisted, and after years of indefatigable work, he was able in 1822 to announce the decipherment of the tablet as well as a system for reading hieroglyphic script.

In the meantime, Egypt was taken over by Mohammed Ali, who became Pasha, or viceroy, for the Turkish. After having put down the Mameluke military caste, he initiated more intense relations with the European powers, trying, through them, to consolidate his own power. Conscious of the fact that the greatest wealth of the country lay in the exploitation of its agricultural resources, Mohammed Ali favored the entrance of European technicians in order to increase agricultural production. And once having entered into the European commercial circle, Mohammed Ali was pushed into introducing the cultivation of cotton on a large scale (a policy that bore fruit later as a result of the Civil War in the United States, where Europe had been obtaining most of its cotton). But if this placed the country in the center of European attention, it also forced Mohammed Ali Pasha to inaugurate a costly policy of sustaining Egypt's international prestige. This led to increased taxes which became a disastrous burden for the already poor lower classes.

Egypt thus became an ideal place for exploiters and adventurers who wanted to get rich with the government's support. And on the wave of privileges conceded to Europeans — above all, those coming from the nations most involved in Mohammed's policy — there emerged the first crest of modern Egyptological excavations. Places like the Thebes and Sakkara areas were sources of material that could easily be sold in Europe to rich collectors or to connoisseur kings. Therefore the archaeological excavations of the first half of the nineteenth century were almost exclusively a search for objects with obvious commercial or museum value. The publication of the *Description*, as well as Champollion's sensational achievement, had made pharaonic Egypt extremely popular in cultivated European circles, especially in France; Chateaubriand, Flaubert, and Gautier all gave special attention to the pharaonic civilization. Buying Egyptian artifacts meant being fashionable, enlightened, and aware of the progressive tendencies of the century.

Among the most noted speculators — despoilers might be a more fitting word — were Bernardino Drovetti, the French Consul, and Henry Salt, the British Consul. Salt's chief agent in the actual search for remains was Giovanni Belzoni, a six-foot six-inch Italian and professional strongman. Some of Belzoni's most important operations included the discovery of the inner tomb chamber of the Chephren pyramid, the cleaning and surveying of Seti I's tomb in the Valley of the Kings, and the cleaning of the great temple at Abu Simbel, which at that time was completely covered with sand. Drovetti, meanwhile, had been assembling remains and offered his collection to France, but the offer was turned down. It was then bought by the King of Sardinia in 1824, thus creating the nucleus for the first systematic Egyptological collection in the world, and still one of the most important — the Egyptian Museum in Turin. Champollion rushed to Turin as soon as he heard of the acquisition, where he was once again able to verify his decipherment of the hieroglyphics. On his return to Paris, Champollion succeeded convincing the government to buy the Salt collection, which then went to the Louvre. Chosen as curator of this new collection, Champollion was finally able to raise enough money to realize his dream of an expedition to Egypt in 1828.

It is beyond our means here to describe in detail the impressions the great Frenchman must have had of the land of the pharaohs. It is enough to realize that after almost two thousand years, he was the first man able to read the ancient Egyptian inscriptions. The history of ancient Egypt was opened up to him, and he was able to formulate the history and chronology of the pharaohs, as well as a grammar of the ancient Egyptian language, work that even today amazes us with its lucid formulations. The intensity and ardor with which Champollion dedicated himself to his studies, amid difficulties and obstacles of every kind due to the rivalry and envy of his colleagues in the French Academy and of those who dealt commercially in antiquities in

Egypt, literally consumed him. In 1832, after returning to Paris, he died of apoplexy at the age of forty-two.

But we must stop at this point. Not because the history of Egyptology has not had great moments or scholars since its beginnings in the first half of the nineteenth century but because we feel that the figure of Champollion is exemplary in so many respects. From the scholar's point of view, he brought to his work both seriousness and knowledge, as well as honesty and enthusiasm. From the point of view of the archaeologist, he brought a vivid and concrete interest to the problems of the monuments, setting the basis for what later became the formal regulation of the excavations. (This must be credited to Auguste Mariette, the French scholar who in 1858 persuaded the Egyptian government to found its official Department of Antiquities.) And, finally, Champollion seems exemplary from the point of view of the sensitivity and understanding he had for the modern Egyptians. It seems most fitting to end by suggesting that all who visit the land of the pharaohs and pyramids or who aspire to appreciate its ancient monuments and culture might well keep Champollion, his work and his attitudes, in mind.

CHRONOLOGICAL CHART

Only the principal kings are listed as individuals, and the names used are those by which they are generally best known. The overlappings in time reflect a divided Egypt or rival leaders.

EARLY DYNASTIC PERIOD

First Dynasty (c. 3100-2890 B.C.)
Narmer (Menes)
Followed by about 7 kings

Second Dynasty (c. 2890-2686 B.C.)
About 10 kings

THE OLD KINGDOM

Third Dynasty (c. 2686-2613 B.C.)
About 5 kings, including Djoser

Fourth Dynasty (c. 2613-2494 B.C.)
Sneferu
Cheops
Redjedef
Chephren
Baufre
Mycerinus
Shepseskaf
Dedefptah

Fifth Dynasty (c. 2494-2345 B.C.)
Userkaf
Sahure
Neferirkare Kakai
Shepseskare Isi
Neferefre
Nyuserre
Menkauhor Akauhor
Djedkare Isesi
Unas

Sixth Dynasty (c. 2345-2181 B.C.)
Eight kings

Seventh Dynasty (c. 2181-2173 B.C.)
Nine kings

Eighth Dynasty (c. 2173-2160 B.C.)
Six kings

FIRST INTERMEDIATE PERIOD

Ninth Dynasty (c. 2160-2130 B.C.)
Princes of Herakleopolis

Tenth Dynasty (c. 2130-2040 B.C.)
Princes of Herakleopolis

Eleventh Dynasty (c. 2133-2061 B.C.)
Inyotef I
Inyotef II
Inyotef III

THE MIDDLE KINGDOM

Eleventh Dynasty (c. 2133-1991 B.C.)
Mentuhotep I
Mentuhotep II
Mentuhotep III
Mentuhotep IV

Twelfth Dynasty (c. 1991-1786 B.C.)
Amenemes I (1991-1962)
Sesostris I (1971-1928)
Amenemes II (1929-1895)
Sesostris II (1897-1878)
Sesostris III (1878-1843)
Amenemes III (1842-1797)
Amenemes IV (1798-1790)
Sobkneferu (1789-1786)

SECOND INTERMEDIATE PERIOD

Thirteenth Dynasty (c. 1786-1633 B.C.)
Many kings, some merely vassals of Hyksos

Fourteenth Dynasty (c. 1786-1603 B.C.)
Seventy-six kings

Fifteenth Dynasty (c. 1674-1567 B.C.)
The Great Hyksos rulers

Sixteenth Dynasty (c. 1684-1567 B.C.)
Eight Hyksos chieftains, evidently contemporaries of Great Hyksos of Fifteenth Dynasty

Seventeenth Dynasty (c. 1650-1567 B.C.)
Princes of Thebes, including Kamose and Ahmose

THE NEW KINGDOM

Eighteenth Dynasty (1567-1320 B.C.)
Amosis (1570-1546)
Amenhotep I (1546-1526)
Tuthmosis I (1525-1512)
Tuthmosis II (1512-1504)
Hatshepsut (1503-1482)
Tuthmosis III (1504-1450)
Amenhotep II (1450-1425)
Tuthmosis IV (1425-1417)
Amenhotep III (1417-1379)
Amenhotep IV (1379-1362) (Akhenaton)
Smenkhkare (1364-1361)
Tutankhamon (1361-1352)
Ay (1352-1348)
Horemheb (1348-1320)

Nineteenth Dynasty (1320-1200 B.C.)
Ramesses I (1320-1318)
Seti I (1318-1304)
Ramesses II (1304-1237)
Merneptah (1236-1223)
Amenmesses (1222-1217)
Seti II (1216-1210)
Merneptah Siptah (1209-1200)
Tewosret (1209-1200)

Twentieth Dynasty (1200-1085) B.C.
Sethnakhte (1200-1198)
Ramesses III (1198-1166)
Ramesses IV (1166-1160)
Ramesses V (1160-1156)
Ramesses VI (1156-1148)
Ramesses VII (1148-1147)
Ramesses VIII (1147-1140)
Ramesses IX (1140-1121)
Ramesses X (1121-1113)
Ramesses XI (1113-1085)

LATE PERIOD

Twenty-first Dynasty (1085-945 B.C.)
Princes of Tanis

Twenty-second Dynasty (945-730 B.C.)
Princes of Bubastis

Twenty-third Dynasty (817-730 B.C.)
Princes of Tanis

Twenty-fourth Dynasty (720-715 B.C.)
Tefnakht
Bochchoris

Twenty-fifth Dynasty (751-656 B.C.)
Ethiopian Princes

Twenty-sixth Dynasty (664-525 B.C.)
Princes of Sais

Twenty-seventh Dynasty (525-404 B.C.)
Persian Emperors

Twenty-eighth Dynasty (404-399 B.C.)
Amirteo

Twenty-ninth Dynasty (399-380 B.C.)
Three kings

Thirtieth Dynasty (380-343 B.C.)
Three kings

Thirty-first Dynasty (343-332 B.C.)
Persian Emperors

PTOLEMAIC PERIOD

Occupation of Egypt by troops of Alexander the Great (332-323 B.C.)

Succession of fifteen Ptolemies (323-30 B.C.)

Romans take over under Octavian (Augustus) in 30 B.C.

RECOMMENDED READING

There are so many books about the ancient Egyptians that the problem is to find the ones best suited to a reader's particular level and interest. This list is merely a selection of books that might well complement various aspects of this volume. They have also been chosen on the basis of accessibility — their price, their recent printings, and their attempts to communicate with the general public.

Alfred, Cyril: *The Egyptians*. Praeger (New York, 1961)
Badawy, A.: *A History of Egyptian Architecture*. (2 vols.) Univ. of Calif. Press (1966-68)
Bratton, Fred G.: *A History of Egyptian Archaeology*. Crown (New York, 1967)
Cottrell, Leonard: *Life Under the Pharaohs*. Holt, Rinehart (New York, 1960)
De Cenival, Jean-Louis: *Living Architecture: Egyptian*. Grossett & Dunlap (New York, 1970)
Desroches-Noblecourt, Christiane: *Tutankhamen*. Doubleday (New York, 1965)
Edwards, I.E.S.: *The Pyramids of Egypt*. Penguin (Baltimore, 1961)
Erman, Adolph: *The Ancient Egyptians: A Sourcebook of Their Writings*. trans. by Blackman. Harper (New York, 1966)
Fairservis, Walter: *Egypt, Gift of the Nile*. Macmillan (New York, 1963)
Frankfort, Henri: *Ancient Egyptian Religion*. Harper (New York)
Gardiner, Alan: *Egypt of the Pharaohs*. Oxford Univ. Press (London, 1961)
Hayes, William C.: *The Scepter of Egypt*. (2 vols.) N.Y. Graphic (1959-60)
Kaster, Joseph (ed.): *Wings of the Falcon*. Holt, Rinehart (New York, 1968)
Maspero, G.: *Popular Stories of Ancient Egypt*. trans. by Johns. Dover (New York, 1970)
Mertz, Barbara: *Red Land, Black Land*. Dell (New York, 1967) *Temples, Tombs, and Hieroglyphs*. Coward-McCann (New York, 1964)
Michalowski, Kazimierz: *Art of Ancient Egypt*. Abrams (New York, 1968)
Smith, W. Stevenson: *Art and Architecture of Ancient Egypt*. Penguin (Baltimore)
Westendorf, Wolfhart: *Painting, Sculpture, and Architecture of Ancient Egypt*. Abrams (New York, 1968)
White, Jon. E.M.: *Everyday Life in Ancient Egypt*. Putnam (New York, 1964)
Wilson, John A.: *The Burden of Egypt*. Univ. of Chicago Press (1951)

RECOMMENDED VIEWING

Nothing makes the world of the ancient Egyptians seem more real than a visit to the actual sites: they still hold their own among the wonders of the world. The next best thing is a visit to a museum collection of Egyptian antiquities, which offer their own insights and enjoyments.

The United States is fortunate in having three especially fine collections, those at The Metropolitan Museum of Art in New York City, at the Brooklyn Museum of New York City, and at The Museum of Fine Arts in Boston. Canadians have an important collection in the Royal Ontario Museum in Toronto. In addition, there are many other collections throughout the United States — all open, within certain restrictions, to the general public. As the list below indicates, everyone should be able to get to one to start an acquaintance with the remains of this unique civilization.

Arkansas: Little Rock Museum of Science and Natural History
California: Berkeley: Pacific School of Religion, Palestine Institute Museum; University of California, Robert H. Lowie Museum of Anthropology
Georgia: Atlanta: Emory University Museum
Illinois: Chicago: Natural History Museum; University of Chicago, Oriental Institute Museum.
Urbana: University of Illinois, Classical & European Culture Museum
Kentucky: The Louisville Museum
Maryland: Baltimore: The Walters Art Gallery
Massachusetts: Cambridge: Harvard University Semitic Museum
Michigan: Detroit: The Detroit Institute of Arts; Wayne State University Museum of Anthropology
Missouri: Kansas City: Museum of History and Science.
St. Louis: The City Art Museum
Ohio: Cleveland: The Cleveland Museum of Art; The Western Reserve Historical Society
Toledo: The Toledo Museum of Art
Pennsylvania: Philadelphia: The University Museum
Pittsburgh: Carnegie Institute Museum
Virginia: Richmond: The Virginia Museum of Fine Arts
Washington, D.C.: The Smithsonian Institution

INDEX